CIPS STUDY

ADVANCED DIPLOMA IN PROCUREMENT AND SUPPLY

REVISION NOTES

Category management in procurement and supply

© Profex Publishing Limited, 2012

Printed and distributed by:
The Chartered Institute of Purchasing & Supply, Easton House, Easton on the Hill, Stamford,
Lincolnshire PE9 3NZ
Tel: +44 (0) 1780 756 777
Fax: +44 (0) 1780 751 610
Email: info@cips.org
Website: www.cips.org

First edition December 2012

Contents

Preface

Welcome to your Revision Notes.

Your Revision Notes are a summarised version of the material contained in your Course Book. If you find that the Revision Notes refer to material that you do not recollect clearly, you should refer back to the Course Book to refresh your memory.

There is space at the end of each chapter in your Revision Notes where you can enter your own notes for reference.

A note on style

Throughout your Study Packs you will find that we use the masculine form of personal pronouns. This convention is adopted purely for the sake of stylistic convenience – we just don't like saying 'he/she' all the time. Please don't think this reflects any kind of bias or prejudice.

December 2012

CHAPTER 1

Definitions

Purchasing, procurement and sourcing

Purchasing is the transactional process of buying products and services that includes raising and placing purchase orders and paying invoices. There is no forwards or sideways thinking in purchasing: a need is presented to the purchaser whose job it then is to fulfil the need. Straightforward, administrative purchasing is sometimes described as **reactive sourcing**. It is sourcing that responds to events and needs as they happen and is therefore unplanned.

The **purchasing cycle** is a convenient process that brings together the stages expected from a 'conventional' sourcing process. The purchasing cycle arranges the stages involved in the act of purchasing into the sequence in which they are expected to occur. CIPS have in the past used a nine-stage cycle to which we have added a tenth stage – the knowledge and experience captured by the purchaser for his organisation.

Procurement is a wider concept than purchasing. Procurement includes all those activities and processes that refer to and implement the organisation's strategies toward the obtaining of its inputs, as well as the actual acquisition. **Strategic procurement** expands on this to include a role in developing these strategies.

Procurement is sometimes referred to as **tactical sourcing**. It is sourcing that takes place within the tactical decision frame, ie with immediate rather than deferred effects. There is still a reactive element but it exists within and is consistent with a strategic sourcing framework. Resources and processes are allocated to enable it to be managed within the sourcing strategy.

Sourcing can be viewed as an activity within procurement, or an activity which precedes procurement. Sourcing means eg 'identifying and evaluating potential suppliers, engaging with selected suppliers and selecting the best value supplier(s). The outcome of the sourcing process is usually a contract or arrangement that defines what is to be procured, on what terms and from which suppliers.' (CIPS Glossary)

Strategy

Strategies are broad in nature – they are planned decisions that impact in the longer-term timeframe. They affect the organisation as a whole (or at least a significant proportion of it), they can address issues that though not urgent yet, soon will be. They are framed in terms of budgets, policies, hopes and intentions. **Tactics** are narrow in nature – they are unplanned decisions that affect the immediate, short-term timeframe.

Mintzberg suggests that actual, 'realised' strategies are combinations of planned and unforeseen elements. They start with an idealised plan, which changes along the way.

- Intended strategy – the result of a purposeful strategic planning process sourced in corporate objectives
- Deliberate strategy – where an intended plan has been put into action
- Unrealised strategy – not all intended strategies are implemented
- Emergent strategy – sometimes strategies are improvised or created because of unforeseen circumstances during a strategic management process
- Realised strategy – the final, realised strategy results from a balance of deliberate and emergent strategies; no actual strategy will be wholly one or the other

These processes apply as much to sourcing strategy as to any other type of strategy.

Strategic procurement and strategic sourcing

Strategic procurement is a procurement process that aligns with and helps develop the organisation's vision, strategic goals and competitive strategy. Strategic procurement activities typically focus on a range of issues such as the supplier base, negotiations, competitors etc.

Strategic procurement's five key tools are as follows: 1) Aggregation – reduces price per purchase and overall costs by reducing the number of transactions. 2) Categorisation – classification of organisational requirements to promote expertise, market knowledge and innovation. 3) Outsourcing – achieves value from third-party expertise and from reallocating resources internally to core concerns. 4) Relationship management – facilitates information and knowledge exchange with suppliers and key stakeholders. 5) Standardisation – a standard set of policies and procedures for individual users and cross-functional teams.

The *Supply Management Guide to Strategic Sourcing* suggests that strategic sourcing comprises four main elements: 1) Demand management 2) Supplier management 3) Total cost of ownership 4) Sustainability.

Strategic sourcing is concerned with the long term. It focuses on those sourcing actions that will realise results over a relatively long time horizon.

Demand management is about matching supply with demand so that no waste occurs in the supply chain. If demand can also be rationalised or reduced, then so much the better, though this is not a primary aim. Demand is set by the organisation's operational needs, and it is not the supply chain's role to say what these should be, but rather to understand them and develop solutions that will more effectively fulfil them.

Most of the organisation's demand will probably come through its **sales and operations planning** process. This is essentially its downstream supply plan, or how the organisation intends to service the pull exerted on it by its customers.

Demand is serviced with supply which is provided by suppliers. The procurement function's use of the supplier base can be developed through a **supplier management** approach. Individual suppliers within the base can be developed on an individual basis through a **supplier relationship management** approach. This term describes the collection of attitudes, tools and processes that the procurement function uses to proactively improve the service provided by a given supplier.

Supplier segmentation is a useful tool. Categories include:

- **Transactional suppliers** with which the organisation has little or no ongoing relationship. Every supply is on a one-off basis with no expectation of a repeat, even if the supplier has a long history with the organisation. Switching is easy.
- **Performance-managed suppliers** where the focus is on tactical outcomes (delivery, quality etc of the immediate supply) rather than on building a long-term relationship.
- **Relationship-managed suppliers** that are seen as having some strategic value, so are nurtured.
- **Strategic suppliers** that are business critical. They cannot be replaced, they account for a large proportion of spend, or they provide highly volatile (prone to risk) supplies.

Total cost of ownership (TCO) is an end-to-end figure that begins with the first steps in supply market research and extends to disposal costs.

The term **sustainability** is used in both a narrow and a broad sense. Narrow sustainability, for procurement, is about acquiring the organisation's inputs in such a way that its long-term performance is at the very least not compromised, and is ideally enhanced.

Strategic sourcing is a frame of reference for sourcing decisions and activities, whereas a **sourcing strategy** is a structured, consistent approach to a specific, recurring sourcing problem.

Category management

Category management is both an approach to procurement and a way of organising the procurement function. The organisation's inputs are divided into **categories** of meaningfully similar items (different points of similarity will be more or less significant for different organisations), which then form the bases for a collection of end-to-end procurement processes.

It is a top-level framework and process that co-ordinates, guides and sequences other methods such as strategic sourcing and supplier relationship management to satisfy category and organisational objectives.

Category management is the process of managing a collection of categories; **category sourcing** is the application of strategic sourcing to a particular category.

The existence of different categories enables closer tailoring of procurement processes to the different needs of different types of organisational input, and allows category procurement personnel to develop substantial expertise in the needs and detail of their category.

Mitchell makes the sweeping distinction that category management is *broader* than strategic sourcing. Category management is an **organisational philosophy** that permeates and organises its activities and attitudes. Strategic sourcing is a focused, technical, tool-driven supply chain activity occurring within the strategic decision frame.

An **account** is an established supply relationship between a supplier and a customer. **Key accounts** represent sufficiently significant amounts of activity to warrant being treated differently from other accounts. **Strategic accounts** are ones without which the organisation cannot operate successfully in the longer term. This may be because of the volume or the criticality of the supply that they represent.

From transactional purchasing to strategic sourcing

A **procurement category manager** is responsible for specific categories of spend. All the suppliers they deal with will come from those categories. By contrast, a **procurement account manager** is responsible for specific suppliers, and not necessarily all of the suppliers active within the categories that those accounts belong to. A customer account manager is trying to grow the activity with the customer accounts for which they are responsible, and to introduce new accounts to their organisation. They want to increase output and make the organisation more effective.

Approved suppliers – an approved supplier is a pre-qualified option in the supply market and is known to meet certain preconditions for supply. Any resulting business is still carried out on a transactional basis, though it may be more frequent.

Preferred suppliers – an approved supplier with some form of relevant differentiation from other suppliers, eg experience, performance, history with the organisation, third-party certification such as ISO accreditation.

When moving away from transactional purchasing the first difference is that comparatively little happens after the supplier has been chosen. In a strategic process all that should be left to do at that point is straightforward administration and monitoring. This transition from transactional to strategic sourcing is often mapped onto 'relationship strength' models.

OWN NOTES

OWN NOTES

CHAPTER 2

Categorising Expenditures

Cost analysis

Categorisation processes typically start with **costs**. Costs, variable costs, fixed costs, semi-variable costs and/or step costs can be categorised according to how they relate to the organisation's level of activity within a specified period of time. The length of the time period and its position in the calendar may influence which category a given cost falls into.

Costs can also be categorised according to how strongly they can be attributed to specified purposes.

- **Direct costs** – directly linked to a specific unit or aspect of the organisation, such as a person, product, service, department or location.
- **Indirect costs or overheads** – spread over a number of identifiable units or aspects. They are costs that cannot be identified directly with specific products or services

Some costs relate to the delivery of the organisation's products and services, whereas others are part of the expense of running the organisation.

- **Product costs** – costs identified with the organisation's products and services.
- **Period costs** – costs treated as expenses incurred during the period and not related to product or service delivery.

In principle, all of the costs incurred in inputting materials into the organisation's production processes should be included in its materials costs. There is a cost-benefit judgement to be made, however. If the costs of meticulous cost allocation outweigh the benefits, then it is better to roll them into overheads, or allocate them to specific orders, requisitions or cost centres.

Organisations are inefficient. As an example, they sometimes buy materials that they end up not using. Unused materials have no value, and are considered to be **waste**. Waste materials that are sold off, typically at a loss so as to remove the organisation's disposal or storage obligations, are considered to be **scrap**. Waste materials costs are indirect costs; they cannot appear as a direct cost because the materials never reached production.

Labour costs will be direct costs if the organisation can relate them directly and exclusively to the single product, process, activity and so on in question. If the labour costs are spread over a range of jobs, activities and so on, each job must take a share of them, so the costs are indirect. People can be paid in a variety of different ways. This can make cost analysis complicated and opens up options for categorising the costs where otherwise there would appear to be none.

It can be difficult to decide whether labour costs are fixed or variable. A salary is a fixed cost, but the costs of the tasks for which the employee is responsible may be variable since each one, even if it is the same basic task, may take a different amount of effort.

Pareto analysis

Pareto analysis provides an alternative way of categorising costs. The Pareto principle applies in a wide variety of situations. The Pareto principle forms the basis for **ABC analysis**. Pareto is a one-dimensional cost analysis and can produce misleading results.

We can address this by looking at total costs, and so factoring in sourcing risk and its cost implications. It is more useful instead to take our Pareto results as one dimension of a two-dimensional analysis and balance them against some other meaningful factor. A familiar two-dimensional analysis is that of Peter Kraljic.

Kraljic's analysis

Kraljic's matrix is a simple spend segmentation tool that identifies four broad classes of organisational input which it is useful to approach in different ways. Kraljic essentially places the criticality of an item to the organisation on one axis of a four box matrix, and the difficulty of operating in that item's supply market on the other.

Strategic items. The organisation will need to recognise its vulnerability and concentrate on co-operating, collaborating and integrating with its supplier, ie introducing elements of co-destiny to the relationship. Supplier relationships will develop features consistent with the longer term, more strategic outlook, eg continuous improvement, early supplier involvement, innovation, mutual total cost reduction, and sustainability.

The suppliers in the strategic class tend to be at the top end of the Pareto analysis, ie part of the 20 per cent of suppliers that account for 80 per cent of the organisation's costs. The organisation spends a large proportion of its time and effort in developing these suppliers.

Critical items are most often known as **bottleneck** items. These items are difficult to obtain and can seriously affect the organisation's ability to deliver its products or services, but are not intrinsically expensive. The organisation's focus will therefore be on securing continuity of supply; any price premium is essentially ensuring that operations keep going. Total cost is important, including the cost of failure to supply the organisation's customers.

Critical items often consume a disproportionate amount of time relative to their value; their supply markets may be complex, or suppliers difficult to find or deal with. The organisation will want to simplify the procurement of these items or, if possible, design out its need for these items in favour of ones from the other quadrants in the matrix.

Leverage items are sometimes described as **commodity** items. There are many suppliers offering much the same product or service. The organisation has the opportunity to 'leverage' its purchasing power and the competitive nature of the market to gain itself a good deal.

Acquisition items are more usually known as 'routine', 'generic', 'standard' or 'non-critical' items. The organisation needs to be efficient in sourcing these. The items involved are comparatively unimportant. Their markets are highly competitive, with many suppliers and low switching barriers. The organisation needs to pay the most competitive price while maintaining delivery and quality standards. Supplier relationships will tend to be arm's-length and transactional.

There are many variations on the Kraljic matrix. Massin's is specifically mentioned in CIPS resources. Massin essentially maps **sourcing groups** or categories on to a Kraljic matrix that has been modified with some of Michael Porter's ideas. The **CSSB matrix** uses two multi-factor axes to map sourcing groups (SGs).

Massin defines sourcing groups with six criteria: 1) They come from a similar supplier source. 2) They have similar production processes. 3) They have a similar use or purpose. 4) They have similar material content. 5) They have similar specifications. 6) They employ similar technology.

Massin suggests that it is useful to organise similar sourcing groups together in a **sourcing tree.** This is a hierarchy that goes from narrow, highly-defined sourcing groups through several levels of increasingly broad specification before arriving at a 'first-level' category. The idea is that different tools, levels of detail, decision frames and so on will be appropriate at different levels.

Bartolini's scorecard

Andrew Bartolini conceptualises strategic and category sourcing as the building of sourcing 'pipelines', and the process of rethinking and reengineering the approaches to various categories as 'sourcing waves'. With that out of the way, it is worth mentioning his **category sourcing scorecard** as a methodical approach to category definition.

Bartolini's scorecard scores different categories across a set of sourcing considerations. It provides a framework by which those factors can be quantified and compared. The end result is a sourcing score for each category that can be used to prioritise categories for sourcing and to allocate resources.

Internal and organisational factors – this group of considerations is aimed at filtering out any spends that will be difficult to fit into a category approach. It looks at:

- Contract status
- Sourcing history
- Stakeholder engagement
- Number of stakeholders
- Access to spend information

Market factors – this group of factors is based on Porter's five forces, and examines supply market competition. It looks at:

- Level of competition (number of potential suppliers)
- Entry barriers
- Substitute availability
- Buyer's relative bargaining power.

Supplier factors – the factors in this group describe the capabilities and attributes of the suppliers in the specific category. It looks at:

- Highly specialised or unique capabilities
- Supplier profit margins
- Value-added service components
- Level of technical excellence
- Financial stability.

Procurement factors – the factors in this group focus on the procurement process and how the use of a given category impacts the organisation and its outcomes. It looks at:

- Supply assurance risk
- Outcomes, operations or production impact
- Category spend volume
- Estimated savings potential.

Category-specific factors – the factors in this group look at the unique attributes of the category that will determine suitability for category approaches. It looks at:

- Strategic impact
- Category complexity
- Lead time.

OWN NOTES

OWN NOTES

CHAPTER 3

Strategic Acquisition Processes

The CIPS purchasing and supply model

CIPS suggests that **strategic procurement** comprises four activities: planning, formalisation, implementation and evaluation. The supply chain function should be involved in **corporate planning** so that the broadest range of supplier options and alternatives can be considered. The **formalisation** (sourcing) and **implementation** of the procurement correspond to the operational activities of the function and **evaluation** captures performance and learning with which to improve current relationships and processes and to build better ones for the future.

Cox suggests that strategic procurement should be implemented in three broad steps: 1) Value chain positioning (VCP) 2) Market positioning analysis 3) Extended relational competence approach.

There are particular features that will be prominent in strategic procurement approaches. Performance measurement is a core activity as discussing performance with suppliers helps achieve (perceptions of) transparency and fairness and performance measurement is key to realising benefits.

The **CIPS purchasing and supply model** is an end-to-end procurement process model that is both plugged into the organisation's strategic concerns and provides operational best practice methods in making procurements.

The organisation will have an overall corporate strategy from which key operational strategies devolve. Thus the corporate strategy contains, for example, a supply chain strategy. The organisation's supply chain, as we are aware, contains a number of operations and departments each with their own more tightly-focused strategies, and the CIPS model highlights three of these: the purchasing and supply management strategy; the operations strategy; and the distribution strategy.

These three strategies must dovetail with each other, and with the corporate strategy. They should support all the other functional strategies as appropriate.

The CIPS model has its own emphases and advice regarding strategic sourcing analysis, starting with the process and competence analysis which begins by identifying the internal stakeholders, constituents or customers of the organisation's purchasing and supply management function in the organisation. The analysis will include a spend analysis, a supply base analysis and a political analysis,

The organisation should trace how supply, and the value that accompanies it, flows into, through, and out of themselves through **supply stream and value stream mapping**. The organisation needs to be aware of key value-adding stages, vulnerabilities, choke points and other critical stages at which substantial value can be gained or lost. It needs to learn what makes these points work as well as they do, and what could make them better.

This entire process is about generating options, establishing what the organisation could do (given unlimited resources), what it can do (given its starting position), and what it should do – which of its options is the most justified?

Rather than wait for other functions to notify their requirements, the purchasing and supply function should proactively work with other functions to plan their sourcing requirements, and to determine volumes, schedules and priorities. From this they should establish appropriate sourcing plans. Sourcing plans should be owned by people who will drive them forwards.

Acquisition – pre-contract is non-strategic sourcing, the pre-contract steps in a tactical purchasing cycle. There are six sequential stages: 1) Identification of need 2) Procurement plan 3) Marketplace solicitation and development 4) Evaluation and selection of suppliers 5) Receive and evaluate offers 6) Create contractual relationships.

Acquistion – post-contract deals with the remainder of the tactical purchasing cycle. There are four stages which are broadly sequential (they overlap): 1) Contract and relationship management 2) Receipt of the product or service 3) Asset management 4) Lessons management.

The OGC procurement process model

The Office of Government Commerce (OGC) was an independent office of the UK Treasury from 2000 to 2010 (its responsibilities have now been transferred elsewhere). It was tasked with maximising value for money in public procurement, and developed a comprehensive procurement process model. The model is intended as generic guidance, applicable in the broadest variety of situations possible.

The general principles are that all procurement should be subject to competition, value for money includes both whole life costs and quality, sustainability issues can be considered where appropriate and when relevant, and that all procurement should be fair, open and transparent.

- The OCG considers that certain purchases are better approached as **projects**.
- There should be a **business case** that justifies the procurement activity and spend. This is critical to senior management agreement and stakeholder buy-in.

- Your **strategy** should set out the key objectives and justification for the purchase. You should also have a clear sourcing strategy and have considered the options for leveraging existing contracts and collaboration opportunities.
- There may potentially be limited response to a requirement because of its nature or the state of the market. In these cases, the organisation should stimulate the market **(market creation).**
- **Requirements** need to be clear and unambiguous.
- Start the **supplier selection and evaluation** process early.
- Proposal **evaluation** considers every supplier that, at the particular stage, meets all the criteria required of them.
- Match the **contracting process** with the **nature of the purchase.**
- **Evaluate** the financial and qualitative elements separately, then look at the results together and reach the trade-off (if one has to be made) that represents best value for money.
- When awarding the contract consider that unsuccessful suppliers may require more attention than successful ones. You need to retain their interest and goodwill for the future.
- **Close each purchase in a controlled way.** Capture the lessons you have learnt. Analysis should capture how well the organisation and process have performed against aims and projections, especially planned costs, schedule, tolerances, and business case.
- There should be a clear **transition process** from the procurement stage to contract management – it is important to ensure your organisation understands and fulfils its obligations so as not to delay or derail implementation.
- Allocate expert and **dedicated contract management** for the term of the contract. You need to have robust procedures, with people to manage the contract. The management provisions should be built into the contract.
- Communication is crucial.

An introduction to strategic sourcing models

Emma Brooks highlights the centrality of strategic sourcing to overall supply chain strategy, and describes the typical issues and tasks an organisation faces in implementing it. She frames this as an eight stage process.

Stage 1 Positioning the function for strategic sourcing
Stage 2 As-is analysis
Stage 3 Mapping the organisation's supply chains
Stage 4 Consolidate data and generate options
Stage 5 Option selection
Stage 6 Sourcing plans
Stage 7 Identifying new suppliers
Stage 8 Evaluation

Category management models

Pierre Mitchell describes how fully-implemented **category management** involves relationship management, communications, programme management, change management and leadership. It almost involves creating intersecting organisations within the organisation, and consequently a large degree of planning and sophistication, and a strategic outlook.

CIPS has its own category management model that divides the process into four phases covering six key activity steps. Each activity comprises key questions which must be asked, and core tasks that the organisation is likely to undertake during the activity. It is a comprehensive model that may be over-specified in many situations. It is up to each organisation to decide for itself which of the elements may be helpful.

Phase 1 Kick-off: *Step 1 Initiate/prepare*
Phase 2 Prepare strategy: *Step 2A Identifying opportunities;*
                             Step 2B Prioritising opportunities
                             Step 3 Prepare/present strategy
Phase 3 Deliver strategy: *Step 4 Implement category strategy/Change recommendations;*
                             Step 5 Maintain
Phase 4 Align/improve: *Step 6 Improve and enhance*

Obrien's model provides more of a process and method that the organisation continually repeats, with clear directions as to what to do when, and what you should expect. O'Brien cautions that there are very many sourcing and category models and that organisations, driven to show they are acting to optimise their practices, may jump from one to the next endlessly. O'Brien suggests that this is the surest route to failure.

OWN NOTES

OWN NOTES

CHAPTER 4

Skills for Category Management

What does a category manager do?

Kay Bayen has investigated 69 skills for their current (2010) and likely future (by 2015) relevance to category management. From her research, Bayen proposes a core skill set for category management and notes that 35% of these are at present under-developed in many supply chain managers. This skill set would support a category manager, whom she describes as being concerned with:

- Value generation
- Cross-functional collaboration
- Alignment of corporate purchasing initiatives with internal users
- Risk management
- Getting indirect spend under control
- Optimising and developing the supplier base
- Sustainability and responsible sourcing
- Developing talent, the organisation, and processes.

Tony White identifies ten skills divided into three groups. His research indicates that these groups are not equally important, but are weighted. That is, category management success is:

- 39% Strategy success
- 36% Relationship management success
- 25% 'Domain' (technical) expertise success.

CIPS highlight technical skills – financial management, cost analysis, supply chain analysis, supply base research, sourcing processes, risk management, legal aspects, negotiation and behavioural skills – communication, influencing, working with teams, cross-functional working, acting as a change agent.

Technical skills

Technical skills are also referred to as hard skills. They concern matters where the data is unambiguous and definitive answers and courses of action are possible. Category management and strategic sourcing are both highly technical activities. Decisions are optimised through behavioural skills, but they are made on facts; options are opened with behavioural skills, but they are identified with technical skills. Behavioural skills may provide the drive for achieving category management or strategic sourcing, but it is technical skills that will map the route to getting there.

Financial management in the procurement and supply chain context concerns the function's need for and use of financial resources. This stewardship extends beyond short-term budgeting and control, and into long-term planning and decision-making.

Cost analysis is a fundamental tool in financial management. A traditional view is that the supply chain function spends money and incurs costs; it is a conspicuous drain on the organisation's financial resources, and can only add value by cutting costs. That is a non-strategic, disjointed viewpoint. The truth is that every function contributes to costs, and every function contributes to revenue. However no function is in a better position to understand and control costs, so **cost analysis** is a central part of what the supply chain function does.

Standard costing is the control system that tracks and analyses variances from standard or budget costs. This enables cost control by setting cost standards for each organisational operation, comparing actuals with standard performance, analysing and reporting variances, and investigating significant variances to take appropriate corrective action.

Variance analysis is the 'evaluation of performance by means of variances, whose timely reporting should maximise the opportunity for managerial action.' So this will have its part in the extensive performance management component of category and strategic sourcing approaches. Variance analysis breaks down a variance to establish: 1) How much is due to non-standard use of resources 2) How much is due to non-standard cost of resources.

Whole life costing (WLC) means costing an organisational input on the basis of costs incurred over its entire existence within the organisation.

The supply chain as a collection of assets is the 'inventory' view of the supply chain – what assets do we have, where are they, what are they doing, and how do they inter-relate? It gives a static picture that does not tell us anything about what has happened or will probably soon happen. It provides a snapshot of a current state that is easy to take in and may reveal important information that is otherwise obscured by movement and activity in the organisation.

The supply chain is also a collection of processes – things that are getting done. These all need to be designed, understood, controlled and joined up. Croxton *et al* describe eight core supply chain processes likely to be found in any organisation.

The supply chain exists to supply, to meet a demand created by an end-user. Supply chains are commonly seen as comprising four types of flow: 1) Materials and services 2) Information 3) Finance 4) Value.

The **Supply Chain Operations Reference model** (SCOR) is a well established and widely known model. It allows the organisation to represent, analyse and configure its supply chains. The SCOR-model is a **reference model**. It is a tool for describing how supply chains work, and provides no prescriptions for improving them.

Before a category manager or sourcing specialist begins working with individual suppliers, he or she needs to research and understand the organisation's supply base. The **supply base**, essentially, is the collected group of suppliers with which the organisation *currently* works. Some organisations consider their supply base to stop at Tier 1 suppliers; others look at Tiers 2, 3 and beyond. From a strategic perspective, therefore we consider all active suppliers in all tiers to belong to the supply base. CIPS identify **sourcing processes** as a key technical skill.

A **consultant** helps an individual, group or organisation (their **client**) to mobilise internal and external resources so as to deal with specific problems.

Internal consultancy is where the consultant and client are part of the same organisation, ie the client is a colleague or stakeholder. It is a complex role, requiring careful relationship management. Internal consultancy can be a successful model for ensuring that supply chain disciplines are pursued throughout the organisation. It can also help the supply chain function to raise its status, credibility and influence in the organisation, encouraging it to develop a list of services to its internal customers, and to market its services on the basis of customer benefits, value for money and business case.

A key aim of **risk management** is summed up in the phrase 'no surprises'. By managing threats effectively an organisation will be in a stronger position to ensure continuity, provide better services and offer value for money. Risk management is the sum of all proactive management-directed activities within an organisation that are intended to acceptably accommodate the possibility of failures in elements of the organisation.

Risk management involves putting in place processes, methods and tools to deal with potential threats that have been identified. This can be as simple as setting financial reserves aside to ease cashflow problems. Similarly, it can refer to ensuring the effective back-up of information systems. In more extreme cases, it can refer to planning for eventualities such as a terrorist attack.

Effective risk management includes early and aggressive risk identification through the collaboration and involvement of relevant stakeholders.

Supply chain professionals should have a working knowledge of all of the **legislative frameworks** in all of the legal jurisdictions in which they operate. 'Working' means enough to get the job done safely: an organisation's activities will vary from jurisdiction to jurisdiction. A working knowledge is also an up to date knowledge – the law is one of the strongest and fastest-changing influences on the organisation.

Supply chain professionals will at least need to be able to read and understand legal documents so that they can competently negotiate and change **contracts**. They should be able to appreciate the implications of each individual clause.

Negotiation is the process by which conflicting parties come together to confer with a view to concluding a jointly acceptable outcome involving purposeful persuasion and constructive compromise.

Behavioural skills

Behavioural skills are also referred to as people skills and soft skills. They are the skills that relate to relationships between people. The various behavioural skills affect the speed at which people make personal connections, align themselves in a common direction, and get each other to recognise, appreciate and further each other's goals.

Communication is the 'first-order' skill from which all other soft skills derive (ie they are 'second-order' skills). Communication includes: observing, listening, questioning, establishing rapport, expressing empathy, communicating assertively, giving and receiving feedback. Second-order skills, in which the first-order sub-skills are applied in specific contexts or for specific purposes, include: influencing, persuading, teamworking, managing conflict, managing people through change, coaching and leading.

Communication is used to **promote** eg a wanted outcome, a vision, goals, values – they are expressed in ways that make them look attractive, desirable and beneficial for the people who will have to adopt or implement them.

Inspirational communication involves the expression of powerful and compelling visions of the future, which appeal to the aspirations of others. Individual, team and organisational motivation depends on a balance between supportive communication and challenging communication.

Daniel Goleman suggests the key attribute is **emotional intelligence** (EQ), 'the capacity for recognising our own feelings and those of others, for motivating ourselves, and for managing emotions well in ourselves and in our relationships'. He identifies five basic components: 1) Self-awareness 2) Self-regulation 3) Motivation 4) Empathy 5) Social skills.

Influencing is the process of applying some form of pressure in order to change other people's attitudes or behaviours. The aim is to secure their compliance (with requests), obedience (to orders), conformity (to norms or expectations), or commitment (to a shared vision).

Terry Gillen distinguishes between manipulative and positive (ethical) influencing. Manipulative influencing uses tactics based on dishonest logic or negative emotion. Positive influencing involves treating people openly, honestly and respectfully.

Rapport is the sense of relationship or connection we have when we relate to another person. We have positive rapport with people we find warm, attentive and easy to talk to; we are inclined to feel comfortable and relaxed with them, or attracted to them. Establishing positive rapport is a skill which can be learned. It is a core skill for influencing because influencing is easier if the other person feels comfortable with you.

Trust is a crucial pre-condition for open, honest communication – which in turn is the basis for positive and deepening collaborative relationships.

Influence draws on a broad repertoire of communication skills. **Persuasion** is influence through rational argument, typically supported by relevant and verifiable evidence. Persuasion is stronger if you can demonstrate objectivity and fairness to both sides of an issue.

Collaboration is the coming together of disparate individuals in the pursuit of (temporarily) compatible goals. It is the essence of **teamwork**; you will need to be able to get teams to work to implement category management and strategic sourcing, to get people to collaborate.

Building a team means resolving conflict between its members. KW Thomas maps conflict handling styles on two dimensions: assertiveness and co-operativeness.

Category management and strategic sourcing embrace the idea of collaborative relationships between organisations and suppliers. Collaboration implies integration and adaptation by both parties. A collaborative approach implies some form of mutual benefit, or sharing of the added value created by the relationship: in effect, a win-win outcome.

Category management and strategic sourcing bring in interested stakeholders and draw on expertise from the entire organisation. Multi-disciplinary or cross-functional (project) teams are brought together so that individuals with different skills and specialisms, competencies and resources, goals and interests, can handle specific category management and strategic sourcing tasks. They are **'task force' or problem-solving teams**, often short-term in nature, and empowered to take action within the limited remit of the task and its terms of reference.

A key source of cross-functional and cross-organisational influence is **networking**: making and cultivating inter-personal contacts. This is what makes consultation, friendliness, coalition and other forms of influencing possible.

The category management approach often entails the organisation making a step-change in its culture and practices. In addition to the organisational and cultural conditions supporting this change, its success depends to a large extent on the attributes and skills of the **change agent** or champion.

OWN NOTES

CHAPTER 5

Understanding the Data

Gaining initial insights into a category

Category management implementation begins a process comprising a sequence of activities that starts with a review of spend information held within the organisation. This provides the first picture of how spend at the organisation works, and what categories may be useful to the organisation.

O'Brien suggests using the **situation, target, proposal tool** (STP) for gathering this information from various sources across the organisation. Define the problem or issue you are trying to understand. This frames the process. Brainstorm and list everything you know about the current **situation** as regards the problem or issue as you have just defined it. Sort the results from the brainstorming into some suitable categories.

Decide on the outcomes, positions and resolutions you want to result from this process. These are the **target**. Targets should be well-defined and 'SMART'. Decide on an action by which you will achieve the target – this is the **proposal**. You can also **plan** out the action and determine the **benefits** that will result. This will give you an 'STPPB' tool.

We are seeking to answer the following questions.

- What have we bought in the past and what do we need in the future?
- How much did we buy in the past and how much do we need in the future?
- Who buys this and why and how do they use it?
- Are we buying the right things?
- What scope is there to buy something different that fulfils the same need?
- Are there any opportunities for improving efficiency in the way we buy and use this category?
- Are there any technological advances now or coming that will present opportunities to us?

Often the move to category management will not only necessitate a re-examination of the spend data and what is required for the organisation, but also an examination of the existing procurement mechanisms and contracts that support product and service procurement in the organisation. These may need to be de-constructed to learn what is being procured, and also to facilitate exit management with existing contracts. A lot of effort will go to understanding both the items supplied in individual contracts and the associated spend.

Demand patterns for category groups

O'Brien's contribution to the problem is his **Day One analysis** (ie how things look right at the start of the category management process). This maps the products and services procured on to a grid reflecting four generic buyer-supplier relationships.

- **Generic** – commonly specified products and services for which there are many customers and suppliers.
- **Tailored** – products or services made uniquely for the organisation. There are likely to be many suppliers, but by definition only one buyer. There will be implications on what is being sold with regard to process and capabilities.
- **Custom** – a product or service is made specifically by one supplier for one buyer. The uniqueness will bring specific capacity, capability and legal issues with it.
- **Proprietary** – a supplier that has achieved and protected unique features in what they supply, but within a category that possesses many buyers.

Strategies are about having a long-term perspective, whatever that may mean in a given industry. Strategic sourcing and category management necessitate that the supply chain function look as far forward as the organisation's strategic planners, which may mean mastering a new set of forecasting tools and learning to deal with a larger amount of forecasting uncertainty.

Strategies and plans cannot exist without **forecasting**; it is forecasting that grounds them in reality and maps out the terrain through which they determine the route.

Forecasts should be **decision-useful**; the forecasts you make should be the ones that generate the most useful information in making a decision. They should be relevant – they make a difference to the decision; they predict and/or confirm and are a faithful representation – they match reality; are complete, neutral, and error-free. Decision-usefulness is improved when forecasts are: comparable (enable comparisons), verifiable, timely, and understandable.

In forecasting, a **trend** is a consistent pattern that has been in place for some time and is likely to continue into the foreseeable future. Trends can be complicated. Few are permanent, and events may happen at any time to change their behaviour. Trends reinforce or cancel out each other. Factors that influence trends include seasonality, business cycles, events etc.

Causal relationships are useful in identifying trends. Few trends are completely self-contained and independent. Where a trend is affected by another, it is said to be **dependent** on it. Trends may affect each other and so be mutually dependent. They may not affect each other at all, and so be independent.

Quantitative forecasting is based on measurable numbers and other hard evaluation methods, and is strongly objective.

Qualitative forecasting is based on opinions, instincts, experience and other soft evaluation methods, and is much more subjective. It is better at dealing with uncertainty and the unexpected.

Primary data: data collected by you, directly and according to your own plan.

Secondary data: data collected by someone else, for their own purposes, and bought in by you.

An important part of creating sourcing strategies, category plans and indeed understanding the categories natural to the organisation is to review and understand its **business requirements**. These essentially identify what we need – they describe the product or service we require, its specification, the required lead time, delivery requirements, target price and so on.

O'Brien organises the organisation's business requirements into a step-by-step analytical process that he labels **RAQSCI**. Each step in the process builds on the ones preceding it.

- Regulatory requirements
- Assurance of supply requirements
- Quality requirements
- Service requirements
- Cost requirements
- Innovation requirements

Business requirements are central to the entire strategic sourcing or category management process, and will: influence the development of the evaluation criteria for selecting the sourcing options; support the development of the supplier selection criteria; form the basis of negotiation strategy as these drive the negotiation outcomes; become the basis for the contracts awarded after any competition or interaction with the market; ground the performance of the suppliers delivering the products or services as they will point up performance measures; become the basis for ongoing management of suppliers and categories; and be the trigger for reviews of categories in the future.

Current contracts, suppliers and terms

One of the most challenging areas to understand, not only in terms of finance, but in terms of actually determining what is currently happening, is the organisation's existing **contractual landscape** with its supplier base.

Not many organisations are centrally organised in respect of procurement, but even when they are it is unlikely that they possess a full knowledge of all the commercial arrangements with suppliers and the terms under which they are conducted.

As full an understanding of the existing organisational commercial landscape as is possible is needed before starting any category management process.

If there is no comprehensive contracts register or supplier record, this needs to be established through data gathering. A clear understanding of the terms and conditions that are in existence within the organisation is of vital importance in order to determine the value extracted from existing contracts by virtue of the terms applied; to ensure that there is compliance across the organisation to the terms and that value is being gained and/or liability is not being attracted through misdemeanour and to ensure that default remedy and exit clauses are understood if there are to be changes to the contract through negotiation or re-competition.

There may be a need for early exit if other deals are more beneficial, so clarity of the organisation's position would be vital in these circumstances.

Market trends

Organisations need to know what is happening in the markets that they buy from as this affects the behaviour of the suppliers within them and the buyers operating amongst those suppliers.

Undertaking this activity is not easy as there are many suppliers, products and services that make up a market place, and they reach far and wide. It also depends on the designation of the category and the degree to which this is broken down in the terms of market place as to how complex the task will be.

For commodities, trend information is important as these markets are driven by forces based on supply and demand, often at the global level. Regulatory bodies affect market activity. As organisations will have little or no influence on the pricing, it is important that trends are understood so as to anticipate price movements and consequently strike good deals. Understanding market trends and the impact such trends have on each category, or on individual products in categories, enables effective modelling of categories and effective market management.

Having a trend focus can ensure that you buy at the right time and in the right way to minimise exposure to price hikes, and to optimise buying position. This area is important and requires attention, and should be seen as **commercial intelligence** to determine when and how to buy.

OWN NOTES

OWN NOTES

CHAPTER 6

Preparing for the Process

Requirements for the preparation of sourcing plans

Data on our organisation's commercial landscape and the utility of the products and services it procures, combined with our demand patterns and ability to exert leverage in respect of them, will provide us with an **opportunity analysis** – essentially a way of prioritising our attention.

O'Brien uses the opportunity analysis to prioritise categorisation efforts to the most promising areas. It is also a very important tool in placing a hierarchy around categories in the two distinct expenditure types of direct and indirect expenditures.

The opportunity analysis offers a quick route to determining whether it is worth mobilising a team to take on improvement in certain categories based on two factors: 1) Potential benefits 2) Ease of implementation. There are two aspects to ease of implementation: ease to effect the change within the organisation commensurate with the likely levels of resistance from stakeholders or users and the process or system changes that would follow that change; and ease in the market place.

The assessment of these factors provides guidance for developing prioritisation and a **hierarchy of categories**, ie the order in which to tackle them.

The other factor in the opportunity analysis is the potential **benefits** gained. One commonly intended benefit is savings through reductions in costs or prices. The two are not necessarily the same, and may sometimes be traded off against each other.

The concept of **value** is important. What are we getting in the round for a given price? It may be there are added features of reliability, functionality, reassurance or prestige that you would not get with other products. However, the buyer's perspective on value is important as it will shape how we proceed to buy. The supplier's perspective on value is to find aspects of value that they think the buyer will respond to, and lock them into their offer.

Total cost models for category management

We are interested here in data that helps us to interpret the current and likely future situations regarding our business requirements so that we can determine the best sourcing approach for our organisation. It is important to determine which specific categories we should prioritise for this treatment.

Challenging the difference between price and cost is one of the key tasks in procurement. The tool we use here is a 'should-cost' analysis – the **purchase price cost analysis** (PPCA) – but it is not suitable for every scenario. O'Brien indicates that its suitability is all to do with power in the exchange with the market; weak buyer power will not allow much room for negotiation on the price versus cost debate.

The analysis should extend out across the entire supply chain eg to your suppliers' purchases.

Having identified cost reduction as a key benefit, we need to recognise that there are other significant benefits which must not be overlooked, eg those stemming from efficiency gains, reduced risk or added value in the supply chain. By looking at benefits and ease of implementation, the opportunity analysis provides the ability to assess the scale of these gains and how difficult it would be to effect any improvement to a given category.

Portfolio tools in category management

O'Brien's variation on the **Kraljic portfolio analysis** is a key tool. It indicates to us where our leverage lies in the range of products and services our organisation uses. By interpreting our findings from using it, we will better understand what we need to do to apply the leverage available to us to its best effect.

O'Brien explains that there are three key steps to using the Kraljic portfolio matrix.

*   Classify using portfolio matrix.
*   Assess the strength of the organisation's position in the marketplace.
*   Determine the required strategic response – either Exploit, Balance or Diversify.

Stakeholder needs analysis

We need to be sensitive to the needs of stakeholders. **Stakeholders** are those individuals and organisations who have a *legitimate* interest or **stake** in an organisation, process, project or decision. '*Stakeholders are those individuals or groups who depend on an organisation to fulfil their own goals and on whom, in turn, the organisation depends.*' Equally, a stakeholder of an organisation is an individual or group who is either harmed by the organisation, or whose rights can be violated or have to be respected by it.

Categorising stakeholders often helps us understand their interactions with the organisation.

*   Internal stakeholders – these are members of the organisation who operate within its boundaries.
*   Connected stakeholders – outside the organisation, but with a significant stake in its activities, frequently through formal ties such as contracts.
*   External stakeholders – the wider range of groups who are less directly affected by the organisation's activities and their results.

We use **stakeholder analysis** to meet stakeholder needs. The sort of questions that may be asked include:

- Where does your organisation create stakeholder value?
- How can you do that better?
- Can you eliminate or reduce focus on processes which do not add stakeholder value?

Identifying and reaching out to stakeholders are key in the category management implementation process. It is important that stakeholder needs are unambiguously documented in the stakeholders' own words so that no misinterpretation or misunderstanding results and a meaningful agreement can be achieved. Stakeholder needs should be reviewed, constraints should be identified, the determined needs should be realistic, the findings should be documented and, most importantly, approval from the key stakeholders should be obtained in writing.

Cross-functional teams

Category management is built on processes, systems and, above all, *people*. Procurement is not simply an organisational function; it is 'a competence, the ability to structure a deal, understand a commercial environment and create a solution to a business problem. To effect this in a business environment, you need good quality people or 'talent'.

Organisations will typically draw together teams from across their operations to lead, drive and achieve strategic sourcing and category management initiatives. The people involved in these teams will rarely be devoting all of their time to them, but will concurrently be working in their usual roles in their usual functional workplaces. This is a benefit and a strength: it embeds the strategic sourcing or category management initiative in the wider life of the organisation. Any initiative will have to feature the collaboration of all departments and functions other than procurement, and this is a head start.

- Appropriate executive sponsorship is essential; it challenges and reduces resistance.
- Managers of staff members seconded to the team will want to know how the initiative affects them, so be prepared for this.
- Do not be surprised if some managers blame time lost to the initiative for sub-standard departmental performance.
- Market the initiative to gain the widest possible organisational buy-in.

Sponsors are important people in a strategic sourcing or category management project, especially during those periods when the improvements or changes that implementation can bring challenge the organisation. The **project leader** is another critical role. The leader is in operational command of the project and works within the enabling framework that the sponsor builds.

Drawing people together from across the organisation is one of the key actions (and arguably benefits) in category management. Getting the right team in place is important; getting a team that can operate as a team is fundamental. Category management will be driven by a **cross-functional core team** that works closely together. This team interacts with an **extended team** containing the sponsor, the **facilitator** who has enabled the project to happen, and stakeholders whose interests and influence lead to them taking a part.

O'Brien suggests that a core team of 5 to 7 people is typical, and this is added to on a temporary need-to basis when particular expertise or experience is required. He also sets out the need for a **team charter** so as to bond the team in terms of activities and goals for their project.

Everybody in a team needs a clear understanding of their purpose for being there. Well-defined team roles:

- Set clear expectations of people; they map participation and involvement.
- Minimise conflict and confusion.
- Maintain structure and consistency when members leave the team and are replaced.

These team roles are not fixed. Within any team, members can occupy more than one role, or switch roles according to need. Effective teamworking requires a mix and balance of all the roles, which between them support task functions and team maintenance functions.

OWN NOTES

OWN NOTES

CHAPTER 7

Supply Market Factors

Industry dynamics, competitiveness and pricing behaviour

Organisations operate within immediate sector or industry boundaries. It is important to understand these to ensure they plan courses of action that will maximise advantage in the future. One tool for this is **industry analysis**. The competition effects surrounding the sector or industry within specific markets are felt more keenly than wider environmental influences.

Porter's **five forces** framework is a well-known tool that supports the assessment of the attractiveness of an industry in terms of five competitive forces: entrants to the market, substitutes for the market, buyer power, supplier power, and rivalry between competitors.

Organisations and the environments they operate in change over time. There can be a danger that organisational change fails to match environmental change; the two lose synchronisation, and the organisation experiences **strategic drift**.

Industries, products, even organisations all tend to follow generally a basic **lifecycle**, from their beginnings to their ends. One thing that an organisation needs to do to understand markets and industries is to determine the lifecycle stage that they have reached. **Industry lifecycle analysis** is a predictive tool, and sourcing strategies require an understanding of an industry's likely future in order to work. The five forces will present differently at different stages in the lifecycle.

A **market segment** is a group of customers who have similar needs that are distinguishable from customer needs in other parts of the market.

Three pricing factors (competition and other market considerations, value as perceived by customers and the cost of production) tend to pull in different directions, and one may influence the price decision more than the others. The 'right' price, that which the market will bear, is determined by supply and demand in the market – what economists call the **price mechanism**.

Baily *et al* suggest: 'Another factor in pricing decisions is how customers value the offering. [It] may include ... reliability, durability, good service and prompt delivery. Perceived-value pricing is based on the customer's perception of relative value rather than on cost.' Different customers have different measures of value, and hence have different preferences concerning it. They will thereby be prepared to pay more for certain features.

Many consumer products and services are very sensitive to price changes, but others show little sensitivity (eg they are an unavoidable necessity or there is little competition in the market). Baily *et al* judge that industrial goods are mainly price insensitive (inelastic), since few of them have true substitutes to which customers can switch easily. This is important information in the understanding of pricing behaviour for category strategy.

Financial data on potential suppliers

Systematic analysis of existing and potential suppliers is a recognised part of supplier management. It is central to setting a sourcing strategy and adopting a category management approach.

The identification of potential new suppliers should be an ongoing process. A financial validation of the supplier is necessary to ascertain whether they will have the basis to deliver the requirements and manage the necessary cashflows in the supply chain to secure supply on your required terms.

The purpose of analysis is two-fold: are they the right supplier to supply your organisation; do they create the right associations for third parties such as customers, other suppliers, regulating bodies?

Assessing financial viability is particularly sensitive but very important, particularly when considering longer-term relationships. It is important to gain a picture of recent and current financial structure and position. There are recognised sources for this, such as company registration authorities, credit rating agencies, and financial markets.

Suppliers should be aware of their standing with the organisation, the basis upon which it was decided, and the potential for their status to change over time. Even so-called approved suppliers should be kept under analysis for improvement, and certainly financial assessment, given the speed and scale of change in economies and markets.

Using requests for information to assess market factors

Uncovering 'breakthroughs' is part of the category management data-gathering phase. **Breakthroughs** are a pillar of category management and are the step changes in understanding and practice that allow us to reinvent our sourcing and procurement. We uncover breakthroughs partly by investigating the market and asking suppliers in the industry what they are currently doing and planning.

We can investigate the market by using **requests for information** (RFIs). These can capture vital activity and supplier innovation and performance that we might otherwise miss. An RFI is an early approach to the market without commitment to solicit information from multiple suppliers and potential suppliers not yet engaged in your business.

An organisation will often use **pre-qualification questionnaires** as part of RFI to ask potential suppliers to disclose specific information affecting their capability relative to a specific bid or need. This is an expected part of competitive bidding. RFIs are often the first stage-gate followed by **requests for proposal** (RFP) and **requests for quotation** (RFQ) as the organisation homes in on the most suitable suppliers.

Internal and external influences on category management

Categories are partly defined as groups of items that ought to be procured with the same sourcing strategy. Sourcing strategies, like all strategies, are products of evidence, assumptions and beliefs concerning the organisation's long-term future, so will be influenced by the organisation's current and projected internal and external environments. There are several tools that you can use to do this. Possibly the most comprehensive version is STEEPLE analysis. Here are some other tools.

- **Risk analysis** is a suitable complementary tool. Rank or score the likelihood that a factor will change and match this to the impact it would have if it did. The higher the likelihood of a change happening, and the greater the impact of the change, the more attention the factor should be given in the organisation's activities.
- The **Boston matrix** (or growth/share matrix, BCG product portfolio) is an analytical tool that uses relative market share (compared to its largest competitor) and rate of market growth to position products within a portfolio. The resulting quadrants (Stars, Cash Cows, Dogs and Question Marks) are used to designate product types, each with its own strategic implications.
- **SWOT analysis** is a commonly used thought-organising and planning tool. Its main usefulness is in locating an organisation in its operating environment and assessing its internal and external capabilities and vulnerabilities. Using a SWOT analysis is a good way of organising all the information you may have gathered through other analyses into a format which makes it easier to assimilate and use. Every potentially relevant point can be mapped to the grid, then all the points in a given box can be consolidated to the key factors and listed as bullets

Corporate social responsibility and sustainability

Organisations have **an impact** upon the world and must **recognise their responsibility** for their actions, the implications and consequences for people and the environment. Organisations are governed by internal arrangements and external regulatory frameworks, but these cannot take account of all stakeholders that might be affected by an organisation's business dealings.

The concept of **corporate social responsibility** (CSR) has both a technical and a philosophical aspect. It is a management tool for gathering together all of the organisation's ethical activities, responsibilities and duties into an integrated framework and a proactive mind-set. CIPS suggest that CSR encompasses four kinds of responsibility.

- Economic responsibilities, the foundation upon which all others rest
- Legal responsibilities, to obey the law and play by the rules of the game
- Ethical responsibilities to do what is right, just, and fair while avoiding harm

- Philanthropic responsibilities, by contributing resources to the community and improving the quality of life

So CSR implies the organisation's responsibility to society (and stakeholders). There are three sets of compelling, driving forces acting to make the organisation behave responsibly: 1) Legal requirements 2) Regulatory requirements 3) Codes of practice to which the organisation has subscribed.

Sustainability is the ability to carry on operating indefinitely, and so is a responsibility to future generations. By implication it implies the reduction of vulnerability and risk, first below the threshold at which an end to operation is inevitable, and then to as low a level as possible.

The idea of **sustainable development** was crystallised and popularised by the United Nations through *Our Common Future*, the 'Brundtland Commission' report published in 1987. The Brundtland characterisation of sustainable development is 'development that meets the needs of the present without compromising the ability of future generations to meet their own needs'. It rests on three sustainable 'pillars'.

- Social development – meeting the needs of all people
- Environmental protection – safeguarding the continuation of the Earth
- Economic development – profit-making *for all* to improve continually everybody's quality of life

The **triple bottom line** (TBL or 3BL) is a balanced scorecard approach to resolving the tensions inherent in the organisation's efforts to reconcile its responsibilities towards people, the planet, and profit, the three pillars defined by the Brundtland Commission. It gives equal weight to the 'bottom line' (to borrow the accounting term) in each of the economic, social and environmental performance perspectives.

It is a way by which CSR can be measured in that the implication is that the organisation's efforts in all three directions should be proportionate to each other. In this way it is also a means by which the organisation's response to the broad set of its stakeholders can be judged.

Supply chain and value chain analysis

Consider strategic **capabilities** and competencies as a function of the sourcing strategy. Fundamental questions need to be asked at this stage to begin any analysis.

- What are the strategic capabilities?
- How do strategic capabilities contribute to advantage and superior performance?
- How do we diagnose these strategic capabilities?
- How do we manage the development of strategic capabilities?

Everything that the organisation is good at or has an advantage in begins with the **resources** it has or can call upon. Resources are physical assets, intangible assets, or capabilities (ie the things it can do). These form the basis for its **core competencies** – the things it does so well that they are worth building its strategies upon.

Johnson *et al* suggest using the **VRIN analysis** (value; rarity; inimitability; non-substitutability) to assess the distinctive resources available to the organisation before analysing its supply chains.

'The value chain describes the categories of activities within and around an organisation, which together create a product or service.' Most organisations are also 'part of a wider value network ... the set of interorganisational links and relationships that are necessary to create a product or service.'

If the concept of value is to be offered to the marketplace by organisations, then they need to understand what activities undertaken within the organisation create that value, and certainly those that do not. Given the increasing propensity for organisations to rely on third parties to deliver their services and products, it is important to understand the value stream flowing through those third-party organisations. This is where the value network concept comes to the fore.

This analysis aids the determination of the real scope of the organisation, links to the operational business, exposes the activities that create value, and highlights stakeholders and their importance across the organisation and beyond. It also uncovers the organisation's capabilities, which provides information to support the sourcing strategy and to prioritise the areas that need attention in order to create competitive advantages and/or reduce losses. O'Brien suggests a simple three-step process: 1) Map the supply chain 2) Identify the **value added** at each step 3) Identify opportunities for improvement or reducing waste in the flow of activities. Consider backward and forward integration.

Analysing supplier perceptions

Suppliers want to maintain and grow the accounts that are important to them; to create a sufficiently well-developed relationship with these accounts such that the supplier feels strong in its position with them. Different accounts are more or less desirable to suppliers, and this will have an effect on the priorities that they have in dealing with your organisation.

The supplier preferencing tool (Development, Core, Nuisance, Exploitable) is about the supplier's perspective, which is analysed as depending on two factors: the inherent attractiveness of the customer, and the value of the customer's business. This tool helps us to analyse why suppliers view our organisation as they do and to assess strategies to change that preferencing.

OWN NOTES

CHAPTER 8

Pre-Planning Preparation

Make or buy decisions

Organisations design their activities to deliver their objectives and core goals. Over time, these change and develop such that the organisation grows, repurposes, and seeks more or different competitive advantages. During this development and growth, the challenge for any organisation is to maintain the effectiveness of its processes in addressing its markets. Therefore supply and value chain analysis are vital in order to highlight the activities embedded within that delivery that mean the most to the organisation's customers and to its success.

The organisation can choose to **integrate** external activities with itself, that is, bring them under its direct control. **Vertical integration** describes situations where the organisation becomes its own supplier or customer. It involves operating at another stage of the value network. There are two options.

- **Backwards integration** – into activities connected with inputs into the organisation's current activities, upstream in the supply chain or value network.
- **Forwards integration** – into activities connected with the outputs of the organisation's current activities, downstream in the value network or supply chain.

It may make sense to bring some activities under closer control. With other activities, it may make sense to loosen control and **outsource** or subcontract them to external third parties. Outsourcing is most commonly associated with support services.

There are outsourcing risks, however. These stem from a variety of sources such as loss of control, accountability, communication with front-line staff, recruiting, security and confidentiality, organisational culture mis-match. At the very least, the organisation has another (long-term) relationship to manage, affected by the complexity and changing nature of the outsourced activity, investment in the relationship, and issues surrounding reliance.

Make or buy decisions apply to all potential procurements, whether they are products, services or raw materials. These decisions have a deep impact on operations and are influenced by a great many different factors.

Switching costs

A key lever for the buyer is the ability to easily move from one supplier to another. The disincentive of doing this, the penalty incurred, is termed the **switching cost**. The ability to switch can be influenced by a number of factors such as the complexity and/or specialist nature of the product or service, the number of suppliers in the market, buying and selling power, flexibility.

Organisations consider whether to work with more than one supplier on each of their requirements, turning to parallel, dual, or multiple arrangements. When an organisation first outsources, it is typically seeking to achieve one or more of the following objectives: increased cost savings, value for money, better service levels, access to best practice, greater innovation. These are not necessarily all found in a single supply partner.

Sourcing options

Ford et al describe **single sourcing** as the arrangement where the organisation chooses a single supplier to provide the entirety of a given supply, and relies on that supplier to carry responsibility for the supply throughout the contract term. The supplier is solely responsible for meeting the obligations of the agreement.

One of the most frequent problems with single-sourcing is that an organisation becomes 'locked-in' to its supplier. It then finds it difficult to create any sense of competition or leverage when sourcing or when seeking to specify new requirements within existing arrangements. An existing supplier may have **incumbency advantages** that make them self-selecting, erecting barriers to other potential suppliers.

Organisations that are aware of lock-in problems have added incentive to select single-source suppliers on sound criteria; relationship matching is crucial. Suppliers that will support the development and creation of cost savings, value for money and innovation are desired.

In **parallel sourcing**, the organisation enters into separate, parallel agreements with different suppliers for different parts of the same supply. Parallel sourcing has the following characteristics: 1) **Choice and flexibility** – it involves competition between suppliers, and avoids lock-in to a single supplier for a broad range of services for a long period of time. 2) **Responsibility** – the organisation's operational risk is higher than in single-sourcing because it delegates responsibility to several suppliers simultaneously. This can make it harder to strike the right deal and ensure that the separate contracts are properly implemented.

The organisation may appreciate the benefits of consolidated sourcing, but consider single-sourcing to be too risky. **Dual sourcing** is an option here. The organisation consolidates its spend to two suppliers. The two suppliers may be treated in the same way on an equal or major-minor split of the business, or they may be treated quite differently.

Multiple sourcing involves using multiple supply sources for the same product or service. This seems the opposite of what category management is about, but it is a valid option.

What category management prevents is *unplanned* multiple sourcing scenarios, where multiple sourcing is not the best option. Multiple sourcing is used to constructively intensify competition.

Cousins *et al* suggest that the organisation should develop a range of suppliers to choose from, and carefully balance capacity constraints with individual supplier performance when placing its orders. Organisations may use reverse auctions to play suppliers off each other and achieve lower prices.

Delivering planned change

Procurement responds to corporate objectives through its functional focus, aiming to for example:

- Provide supplies to match customer needs – eg assure quality, reduce delivery lead times, reduce cost.
- Reduce stocks and improve reliability, eg through more frequent deliveries.
- Introduce early supplier involvement and simultaneous engineering.

The goals and contribution of supply chain management as realised through procurement are considerable. There are clear strategic themes at play for managing strategic change within procurement.

- The need to respond to changing environmental conditions
- Movement towards a proactive role which emphasises the strategic importance of supply chain performance for organisations as a whole
- Strategies for supplier relationships
- Performance-oriented sourcing strategies that control the basic features of quality, delivery, cost and service
- Organisation of the supply function
- Application of information and communications technology to supply chain management activity

Integrating processes between organisational strategy and procurement implies the following: 1) A formal, long-term procurement plan as part of the corporate planning process (or as a component of strategy) 2) Purchasing managers being involved in the corporate planning process 3) Top (boardroom) management integrating the function with the organisation, providing guidance on corporate strategy and direction 4) Strong interpersonal relations between supply chain managers and a supportive chief executive.

Essentially what we seek is to ascertain how procurement, supply chain and organisational strategies fit together, and supply chain management's role in the management of organisational change, such as the introduction of category management or the development of sourcing plans. We want to assess how the procurement process should be placed to deliver planned changes.

Risk planning and mitigation

Risk management is not value-adding, but it prevents value being destroyed. In this sense it is very open to cost-benefit decisions balancing potential loss against certain expense. **Risk mitigation** is the reduction of the chance and/or effects of risk. There is another cost-benefit decision, as different mitigation plans will reduce risk by different amounts. Risk management and mitigation will be targeted against those risks with the greatest effects; less important risks should receive prortionately less attention.

Risk assessment or analysis should take place as early as possible and should be an ongoing concern. Category management institutionalises risk assessment by including a SWOT analysis, but risk management procedures should be more thorough than this.

A common feature of risk management is **thresholds** beyond which risk is considered to become unacceptable. These can be set in many different ways, eg days late, parts defective, lives endangered, money lost and so on. When these thresholds are crossed, risk mitigation or contingency plans come into play. **Risk levels** are generally measured by looking at the chance of happening and the impact should the risk materialise. Risk is often poorly understood; explaining to stakeholders what risks mean will be a key task. A **categorisation system** can be a useful broad-brush device through which to quickly communicate risk and assign priorities.

Risk management is a specialist skill – the category manager needs to be familiar with it, but might not be familiar enough to conduct risk analysis as well as the organisation would like. The organisation may also want some element of scepticism and independence in its risk assessments – things that the category manager cannot provide.

The best risk strategy is to make the right small changes early, so that risks are always at least blunted and ideally avoided.

Literally, **contingency plans** are plans for what the organisation will do should a risk materialise. They cannot, by definition, reduce the chance of a risk as they come into play only once it has happened. Instead, they reduce its effects. Mitigation or avoidance is obviously far preferable. Cost-benefit arguments apply: contingency planning eats up resources, and its upside must more than compensate for that. Contingency plans may be reserved for core-purpose, critical systems and activity, ie **business continuity planning**.

Some risks are accepted – the organisation considers planning against them to be more trouble than they are worth. Risk acceptance is a decision that may have to be defended later; the justification for it should be evidenced and recorded. All other risks are monitored. Monitoring will include review – the organisation will want to spot the early signs of a risk materialising, but also spot changes in its nature, probability and severity.

OWN NOTES

OWN NOTES

CHAPTER 9

Planning the Process

Involving stakeholders in the sourcing decision

The sourcing strategy is a key pillar of category management. It sets direction and scope for the procurement of specified products and services over the long term. A key goal for the organisation in developing its strategic sourcing decisions is to realise high levels of value.

In this environment, the procurement function becomes a primary value generator and must intervene across the entire organisation to achieve its value-generation goals. Procurement must explain the point of its sourcing decisions to create a shared understanding amongst key stakeholders, and to nurture supportive 'category user behaviours' from stakeholders that will help it to deliver value gains and retain them.

The organisation must seek out every possible source of value and co-ordinate them to the best overall effect. Value gains do not just arise from favourable price movements, but also from innovative practices, different product utility, whole life cost management and differing buying methodologies, all of which require lateral thinking encompassing all of the organisation's functions and user communities. Making the optimal sourcing strategy decision is critical, and needs to involve organisation-wide business elements and stakeholder requirements. Stakeholder engagement and buy-in is critical to success.

Porter describes a **value chain**. This identifies the categories of activities at and around an organisation that are co-ordinated to create a product or a service. This model can be used to distinguish those activities and functions that add value and are therefore needed from those that do not and therefore are not. His model exposes the areas where improvement efforts are worthwhile or where costs might be driven out.

If an organisation can be seen as a value chain, then a supply chain is a chain of value chains or, in Porter's terms, a **value network** or **value system.** It is the infrastructure of inter-organisational links and relationships that is necessary to create a product or a service from raw materials. In a value network, organisations (increasingly) rely on third parties to supply products and services to and for them, and these third parties therefore become involved in the value chain too. Their behaviour and performance should not be overlooked.

Stakeholder mapping is the key strategic tool required to commence formal stakeholder engagement. There is no mapping method that is the best in all circumstances; each is more or less useful according to the needs of the situation.

Mapping needs to be broad, not narrow, in the stakeholders included. Other supply chains, services and environmental factors may be impacted by or may influence the product or service delivery with which you are concerned on a given project; a wider net of stakeholders may hold influence.

It is not only the named or known stakeholders that must be planned for in terms of involvement or engagement, but any stakeholder who is a 'touch point' with the product or service. A study of the value chain will identify the touch points and their impacts, and will provide clues as to how to interact with them.

These issues must be understood in developing strategic sourcing decisions. O'Brien suggests that a typical stakeholder map would begin with a **RACI analysis: Responsible, Accountable, Consult, Inform** (which divides stakeholders by their level of engagement, from those most involved to those least involved), and would provide an analysis showing an assessment of the identified participants.

O'Brien identifies four types of relationship with stakeholders. There are those who: *Are against it happening, Let it happen, Help it happen* and those who *Make it happen.*

Stakeholder involvement is an ongoing activity throughout O'Brien's category management process and any other similar process we might examine. Defined roles are set for key players to ensure category management outcomes are met. Some thought should be given to a formal communications plan to convey the relevant information to start the specific activity of planning and developing the sourcing decision-making.

Creating evaluation criteria

An organisation will probably have a number of strategic options open to it. Whatever evaluation criteria are set, these should be transparently and logically arrived at from a justifiable understanding of the organisation's current state, operating environment, stakeholder influences, and the ways in which it may be beneficial for it to move forward.

Evaluation criteria should be founded on the organisation's goals and objectives for the categorisation. These will be set by the category management team from their internal and external analyses, as interpreted through stakeholder factors.

Sourcing strategy options reflect the circumstances in which they were made. It is important to retain detail on how they were determined, on why their recommendations were the most important course of action the organisation could take at that time, and precisely how, in a step-by-step fashion, they were intended to be achieved. Without this information, an organisation cannot meaningfully apply evaluation criteria.

O'Brien sets out an approach for generating sourcing options. Evaluation criteria divide into two fundamental types: business requirement and implementation. O'Brien suggests that a scorecard or matrix is developed early on in the process. A sourcing strategy statement will now need to be developed.

Finalising specifications and contractual agreements

Once the strategic option is chosen, it is good to secure a clearer picture of what is actually required and affirm and agree it. Defining and redefining the business requirements is key to progressing category management sourcing decisions. Basic analysis centred on Pareto-type breakdowns of spend will focus attention on the right items and categories in the first instance, but these should not be under-estimated as tools for further analysis.

Business requirements contain a structured description of what the organisation needs and wants from a category in order to satisfy its objectives. They should be built up initially from the stakeholders' positions on what the organisation is trying to achieve and what actions will achieve these outcomes.

By re-examining the category requirements against the value levers, stakeholders can collectively uncover possibilities for added value and highlight potential other areas for exploration or deeper investigation. 'Why does it need to be this way?' is a key question stakeholders are expected to ask when conducting this activity.

It is at this stage that the sourcing plan can be presented for sign off. Only on completion of this phase is it advisable to proceed to the implementation phases.

Once the strategic approach is determined and the requirements statement agreed, some thought and planning must be given to the preparation of the contractual side of the project. A written contract is always advisable. A formal document will need to be prepared setting out how the external provider should make proposals for the business of the category to be delivered. Such activity and indeed progression through the market activity and buying process create clear legal obligations on all parties involved which need to be understood.

Contractual difficulty between parties can arise as to when a contract is actually formed, so care must be taken when engaging with the market or when members of the organisation are interacting with suppliers, especially in the early stages of engagement.

Procurement personnel are not necessarily legal experts and need to refer to contract specialists. Significant study should be undertaken on contract law separately. However, these basic terms should be understood for category management.

- Offer and acceptance and consideration
- Invitation to treat, invitation to tender/quotation
- Intent to form a contract
- Contracts and purchase orders
- Battle of the forms
- Terms and conditions
- Contractual clauses – exclusion, termination and remedies
- Implied terms – sale and supply of goods and services
- Framework agreements and call-offs
- Letters of intent
- Memorandums of understanding

Formal contract documents should contain a traditional contract, specifications, commercial details (including prices, fees, costs), relationship management details, performance reviews, account planning, and terms and conditions.

The use of confidentiality agreements

An organisation may want to consider using **confidentiality agreements** or **non-disclosure agreements** (NDA) in discussions with suppliers if it believes it will be disclosing commercially valuable information. Confidentiality is usually associated with intellectual property and trade secrets, but can relate to any information that is considered important and needing to be protected against free circulation and exchange (eg it may affect share price).

A confidentiality agreement is a contract between at least two parties that outlines confidential material, knowledge or information that the parties wish to share with one another for certain purposes, but wish to keep secret from all other parties. The parties agree not to disclose the information covered by the agreement, and make themselves subject to legal sanctions should they break it.

If **category management** is deployed effectively, it can maximise profitability through critical targeting of one type of product or service used in the organisation. However, this can only be achieved if category management is adopted as a philosophy and practised throughout all of the relevant functions of the organisation as determined in a strategic plan agreed by all of its stakeholders.

Delivering a category approach within the organisation may require a considerable shift in organisational mind-set, functional structure, and culture. Another key area to consider is the optimisation of legal and business relationships with suppliers, and perhaps other parts of the organisation, to best advance the outcomes procurement seeks in applying category management.

To maintain value benefits downstream and to optimise procurement activity within categories and supply chains, the organisation needs to reconsider its needs as embodied in its specifications and what its short, medium and long-term needs are prior to implementation planning. The organisation must be mapped and a shared understanding developed of the strategic implications of these requirements for the organisation. Such analysis and re-thinking can determine how best to engage with the market to secure the products and services needed and to re-inform the category strategy going forward.

OWN NOTES

9

OWN NOTES

CHAPTER 10

Routes to the Supply Market

Competition and negotiation

Competition essentially means the use of tendering procedures – advertising the requirement widely and inviting suppliers to tender for the business. **Negotiation** means identifying a small number of suppliers and dealing directly with them to agree contractual details.

In the EU, **procurement directives** impose competition rules upon public sector bodies These rules ensure that public sector bodies approach the market in a manner that enables fair and open competition among suppliers and service providers within the EU. In other words, for EU public sector bodies the normal approach to supplier selection is competition rather than negotiation. Features include:.

- **Common procurement vocabulary** – an EU-wide coding system for categories of products and services that might be procured.
- **Competitive dialogue** – a procedure that may be used for complex contracts. Requirements are defined in *output* terms. Purchasers may seek initial proposals from suppliers and then have dialogues with some or all of them in successive stages, prior to requesting final bids from those that can meet the output specification. The capacity for dialogue enables changes to initial proposals not allowed under open or restricted procedures.
- **Framework agreement** – following a competitive process, an organisation may conclude a framework agreement with suppliers against which it awards specific subsequent contracts.

Competition takes time to achieve: time to advertise a need, gain interest, allow suppliers to understand the requirements and prepare a bid. This is particularly important to public sector buyers, who operate under stricter regulations. It is considered important that suppliers have a fair and reasonable turnaround time for their bidding processes.

It obviously makes sense to ensure that there is reasonable time for bidders in all procurement processes. Category management is a time-consuming process and a costly one, but organisational pressures must be resisted and impatient stakeholders and colleagues helped to understand that the necessary time is an investment that will realise dividends later on through improvements that would not otherwise be possible. The focus should be on developing the optimum timescale for a competitive procurement process

The category management skill-set encompasses a methodical approach, knowledge-gathering, insight-forming and innovation, which are all equally good for successful negotiation. A planned strategy will be important, too, to ensure delivery of the desired outcomes. This means answering some fundamental questions about context, aims, challenges and concessions.

Business requirements should *always* be used to drive a negotiation and form the basis of the outcomes that the organisation targets. There is no intrinsic best or worst answer in choosing between competition and negotiation. You may decide that a particular situation should involve elements of both. The individual circumstances will indicate the best path forwards.

An organisation issuing an invitation or request is merely expressing its interest in receiving offers (not its intention to buy) from the marketplace. This is known as an **invitation to treat**. The organisation may accept any satisfactory correctly submitted tender or quotation that it receives. However, it is not under any obligation to accept any of them; it has only expressed an interest.

Invitations and requests

An **offer** cannot change once it is fixed. Once a tender is received by the organisation, then it stands as the offer from that supplier. If the organisation wants to negotiate on that offer its position changes to a prospective buyer making an offer of their own – they have rejected the original offer and are effectively now making a new offer.

There needs to be complete clarity during this process to avoid either party accepting an offer they had not intended to. The status of the invitation or quotation is important as there are implications in respect of when a contract is being made. Contracts are best made in writing, but the process takes place before there is a contract. A contract can be made by actions and through conversations, and not just in writing.

Finding a supplier can be difficult enough in a competitive arena, so putting forward the best information to attract them is key to success. Increasingly difficult questions are asked of increasingly few suppliers as the organisation progresses from RFI to RFP to RFQ (sometimes collectively referred to as RFx). These processes are commonly implemented through the internet now. Computer-based platforms allow suppliers to log in to an e-sourcing tool to access the necessary bid activity and respond in kind rather than phoning or writing letters.

Requests for information (RFI) from suppliers can form part of the data-gathering process or source planning activity. This is a solicitation tool sent to multiple suppliers to gain information about products, capabilities, organisation set-up, facilities etc. RFI activity is not necessarily considered part of a competitive process.

Requests for proposal (RFP) are sent to limited numbers of suppliers who are asked to provide a proposal on how they would meet stipulated requirements. An RFP 1) invites the supplier to bid for business 2) seeks a solution to a problem or need 3) conveys key business requirements 4) is focused on the supplier's experience, qualifications and proposals.

Requests for quotation (RFQ) are used with few suppliers, either on their own relatively low-value and commonly supplied items on a specific proposal and pricing basis, or as a follow-up to the RFP. This time suppliers are asked to provide bids against firm, specified requirements.

The RFP or RFQ process may be known as an **invitation to tender** (ITT). The three are functionally equivalent. For this reason it is important to develop invitations and requests that capture only absolutely necessary information and ask the following questions: 1) Why do I need to know this? 2) How is the supplier likely to respond to this? 3) What format will I need the information from that question to be in in order to evaluate it?

Depending upon the nature of the approach to market and the economic sector involved, there may be preferences, limitations or prescriptions on the approach to market. Within the public sector there may be a requirement either to approach the market on an **open competitive basis** (inviting all suppliers to bid irrespective of their capability), or to use **restricted procedures** which permit the organisation to reduce the number of potential suppliers to a manageable number (eg between five and twenty) that still preserves sufficient competition to return an optimal result from the process.

Supplier selection

Supplier selection needs to build in various points at which the organisation reduces bidder numbers in a consistent, fair and open manner. There are various points at which this can be achieved, the first being pre-qualification. This initial stage permits a 'weeding out' of suppliers who will not be at all suitable to fulfil the requirements on any grounds; they usually cannot meet even the fundamental criteria.

Assuming that more than one supplier has passed pre-qualification, then some suppliers will go through to next-stage evaluation. If only one supplier has passed, no further *selection* criteria are needed, but the remaining supplier still needs to be evaluated for capability, suitability, price and so on. At this stage suppliers receive tender documentation of some kind, ie RFP and possibly RFQ.

Depending upon the nature of the requirement, there may be a need to meet prospective suppliers and have presentations from them on how they would approach the work offered. A third evaluation may be held once the final selection has been made to undertake a final validation of the supplier(s) if necessary. It is concerned primarily with due diligence audit checks around people, systems, operations, facilities, accreditations, and financials. Contract award is then the next step if all is satisfactory.

Reverse auctions

A **reverse auction** literally reverses a conventional auction. Ordinarily, in **forward auctions**, buyers compete for a product or service with increasingly higher bids. In a reverse auction, sellers compete to sell, offering increasingly lower prices.

E-auctions are auctions that take place electronically; they allow an organisation both to sell (forward auction) and buy (reverse auction). They have the legal status of an invitation to treat. Generally, e-auctions are *reverse* auctions. They happen in real time over a limited, scheduled period. During the auction, suppliers (sellers) will make bids and counter-bids, each time lowering the price. At the end of the auction the best offer – ie the lowest price – wins.

Best practice states that an e-auction should be preceded by spend analysis and one or more rounds of RFx so that supplier filtering based on price and non-price factors can be conducted beforehand. Variants of e-auctions include: standard reverse auction, cherry-picked auctions, bundled auctions, cherry Dutch auctions and Japanese auctions.

There are problems in buying like this as clearly the emphasis is on price. The specification and requirements need to be clear and understood prior to the auction so that there can be no ambiguity over what is expected and then delivered. An e-auction is really a non-face-to-face negotiation mechanism. They do not suit complex requirements of a strategic nature where there are few capable suppliers.

O'Brien suggests some factors that must be considered if the organisation is to succeed: lot strategy, specification, price awareness, inviting the right suppliers, selection criteria resources, training and communications.

Joint proposition improvement

Joint proposition improvement is an approach whereby a buyer and supplier work together under their contract to jointly improve performance or to develop the contract to their mutual gain. Generally, this would form part of the category management strategy for an existing provision that requires an upgrade in terms of the service that can be expected under the boundaries and limitations of the existing arrangements. The buyer and supplier should take legal advice to determine the extent of negotiation and change that can be made to the existing contract without infringing competition rules. It is an attractive option if it can be made to work since, mostly, an incumbent supplier will have experience, knowledge and insight concerning the supply; perhaps enough for significant re-engineering opportunities.

The best approach is for the buyer and supplier to jointly develop a plan for the activity within the category or contract to move from its present steady state to the desired improved state over a planned, specified time.

OWN NOTES

OWN NOTES

CHAPTER 11

Implementing the Process

Governance structures

Governance is the manner in which an organisation determines its activities and steers its affairs: whether it is transparent, accountable, methodical, 'by the book'. It is the manner in which the organisation executes category management. This involves planning, management and day-to-day progress measurement until category management objectives have been achieved.

An organisation will have some form of governance structure that binds its people, systems, policies and strategies together. There will be key activities that this structure needs to enable, and a **steering group** at the heart charged with leading the entire programme effectively. Its responsibilities will typically include the following.

- Assuming overall responsibility for the category implementation programme
- Defining objectives, targets and timing
- Ensuring a planned and managed approach throughout; co-ordinating each category
- Monitoring the programme and reporting on progress against plans
- Ensuring the right capabilities and resources are in place to deliver category management
- Initiating and managing communications organisation-wide
- Reporting progress to the executive team

The programme plan, outlining the categories included in the initiative, will be a driving influence behind governance. One of the plan's features will be a timeline of events, targets and milestones. These should be tracked individually, and key ones may be gathered together in a 'dashboard', but there should also be formal, wide-ranging reviews as the programme moves between its key phases.

These **stage-gate reviews** ensure that there is a clear understanding of where the project is in terms of delivery, and act to maintain the timing and pace of that delivery. The benefits to be realised within a category as identified in the strategy should be measured, validated and reported. Benefits will have been planned for right from the start, and their progress through successive stages of certainty will have been tracked constantly until finally they are realised. As we will see when we look at performance measurement, such benefit tracking is a key part of evaluating the success of category management, but also of keeping the process on track.

The steering group needs oversight of what is happening across the implementation of the category management plan. Progress against plan needs to be mapped such that it is easy to determine whether the programme is on track, and to put in place remedies to correct matters if it is not. Reporting is fundamental to the governance structure and must be maintained regularly to keep the plan on track, but also to audit the proceedings.

Every category management programme and implementation will be different and will require different levels of different skills and different types of individuals. Certainly, the right skills and resources must be found in the right quantities when they are needed to achieve the level of output required against the plan. Some training and development will be needed to support and develop the people joining the various teams.

The aims of the programme should be understood across the organisation by the time the implementation stage has been reached, but there is also a need to communicate in different ways across the organisation, especially as the implementation gets underway. There will be a need for direction and motivation, not just explanation, consultation and reassurance.

Deciding on a sourcing transaction approach

A framework that will help to integrate these disparate lines of thought and point the way forward is provided by the Handfield and Straight portfolio matrix that has some similarities with the Kraljic matrix.

Exchanges automate supply by connecting suppliers and buyers electronically. They also connect buyers for **group buying** purposes. Exchanges can be public or private. Exchanges enable more suppliers to reach more buyers, but they do require administration, which is a cost, and collaboration, which some buyers may find difficult given the casual nature of the alliances formed.

Spot buys are the antithesis of strategic sourcing and category management. They are unplanned, needlessly urgent, one-off, needlessly time-consuming, subject to market conditions, oriented towards price rather than cost, and make poor use of the organisation's leverage.

Integrators are third parties to whom the organisation outsources specific procurement and sourcing activities. In this unit's context, the organisation's procurement specialists would contract a consultant to work with them on an unfamiliar category in which the consultant was an expert. The consultant would then manage the activity relating to that category. Integrators allow organisations to concentrate their resources on strategic sourcing, and bring high levels of expertise to all parts of their sourcing efforts, even the low-priority ones.

Relationship management in supply chains

According to O'Brien, the organisation's agenda in category management is as follows.

- To continue the search for value using the value levers concept
- To refine and optimise the business requirements
- To communicate and engage with suppliers
- To innovate in line with what the market can offer and the changing needs of the organisation
- To drive effectiveness by aligning and adapting supplier relationships

The management of suppliers is critical to the organisation in general, and especially to category management. In adopting the category approach, our first goal is to align to the market and how it supplies products and services within our categories. In developing a clear picture of what our usage of the various products and services are, we should then be able to determine what suppliers currently supply to the entire organisation (or at least a significant portion of it). In focusing on categories, there is a danger that we miss the organisational dimension of procurement and supplier delivery unless there is a separate activity focused upon suppliers and the relationships that we need with them.

Supplier relationship management is the process that frames and directs the development and maintenance of relationships with suppliers. It is part of strategic sourcing and category management. It supports the development of close, cross-functional relationships with key suppliers, while at the same time accommodating arm's-length relationships with others.

With this approach, category managers, sourcing specialists or supplier relationship managers work with the key suppliers to develop individual **product and service agreements** (PSAs) to meet both the organisation's and the supplier's needs. These form the basis of goal-setting, contracts, and performance tracking. Performance particularly is a mutual issue: not only the profit impact of the supplier on the organisation, but also of the organisation on the profitability of the supplier.

McIvor notes three potential generic relationship strategies: non-specific contracting; recurrent contracting; and relational contracting.

Non-specific contracting relates to those situations where the supply market is easy and full of suppliers and competition. Buyers' needs are not particularly differentiated. This type of arrangement is driven primarily by the transaction. Relationships are relatively short-term, based on bargaining relationships between independent buyers and suppliers.

The buyer's needs can be quite specific, in which case **recurrent contracting** is appropriate. This involves repeated interaction and moderate investment in the relationship. The reasonable possibility of switching suppliers means that although the buyer invests in order to co-ordinate complex and non-standard processes with the current supplier, this is not allowed to lead to over-dependence on that supplier. Relationship-related assets are, as far as is possible, transferable to a new supplier.

11

Relational contracting means developing a longer-term, collaborative relationship. This is a type of relationship appropriate for critical, competitive advantage building processes. The potential for opportunism is high: there are few potential suppliers; the transaction cannot be fully specified or its elements controlled. The buyer and supplier build value with each other. They invest in assets that create a high level of mutual dependency. Because they are bound in to each other, they resolve difficulties through softer, more social means.

The category management process should result in new relationships and in old relationships being re-established on new terms. There may be an unfamiliar degree of closeness to the new relationship arrangements. These will need to be **embedded** into the organisation and into suppliers.

This is a familiar idea in any change management process: unless a change is wired into the organisation, some people and systems will slip back to where they were before with some parts of the organisation wanting to work one way and others in another, and tension between the two. The organisation needs to consider what mechanisms it will set up to embed its new arrangements. These can include: 1) Training 2) Accreditation 3) Organisational tools that are specific to the new working methods 4) Benchmarking.

Segmentation is about dividing suppliers into tiers of importance in respect of what they provide to the organisation. This permits an assessment of how you should manage them within the tiering. A reflection on what products and services a supplier provides and how these fit your business is a good place to start. O'Brien's Day One analysis can be helpful here.

It is best to use a Pareto approach to segment suppliers in terms of the resources that should be committed to managing them. Only the top tier justifies a fully-developed key supplier relationship management approach of the sort we have been discussing.

The main purpose in managing a relationship with a supplier is to secure improvements. Improvements are best achieved collaboratively. There needs to be joint intent to work together for continuous improvement and added value. Once the segmentation exercise has been done, there may be an awareness of what improvements need to take place.

OWN NOTES

OWN NOTES

CHAPTER 12

Working with Stakeholders

Stakeholder buy-in

The *Supply Management* Guide to Strategic Sourcing explains how the trends in most organisations are towards increasingly well defined organisational units with increasingly deep expertise in increasingly narrow areas of responsibility. This runs against the spirit of strategic sourcing and category management, which by contrast is cross-functional and 'big picture' in nature.

Sourcing and category project sponsors and leaders often have a substantial change management element to their work, involving parts of the organisation that they know little of and which want to know little of them. Category management strategies bring change and there will be resistance to change. Inability to overcome this resistance may affect the realisation of benefits and must be addressed.

One implication is that the entire project team needs to be able to operate well at a strategic level. It will need a thorough understanding of the organisation, to be aligned with the organisation's vision and longer-term objectives and have a deep understanding of what stakeholder and customer needs actually are and will be (not what the organisation believes or wishes them to be).

All solutions should be considered temporary. If we can demonstrate that our new sourcing approach is returning better results on outcomes, getting our colleagues and other stakeholders to accept it and the solutions it suggests should be easier. It widens out the range of sourcing strategies we can contemplate and prepares us for options which, though not yet practical, may soon be. Breakthrough solutions are rarely breakthroughs, they simply reach the point where their realisable benefits become greater than their cost.

Stakeholder buy-in is key to category management success. It is important to seek it from the earliest possible point in the process. Stakeholders are not necessarily reliable or capable of being satisfied. Stakeholder engagement or customer involvement is necessary to stem any antagonism towards the change. People are only too quick to point out weaknesses or failures if they do not own them in whatever small way, or have not been invited to commit to the change from early on.

Much of what has been discussed is input-based engagement. Stakeholders may have output effects, too, on organisational policies, contracts, agreements or post-implementation activities.

12

It is necessary to examine some output-based interaction with the stakeholders and the category management teams. Communication rather than coercion is the main means to reaching and involving stakeholders, but we also need their buy-in. Stakeholders can become involved without feeling convinced and committed. We need to use that same communication for knowledge sharing, to promote and publicise benefits, to involve customers and stakeholders through more proactive decision participation and emotional engagement with the sourcing strategies.

At the implementation stage it is all about turning sourcing plans into reality and making gains. O'Brien suggests formal implementation workshops that communicate as far and wide as possible and celebrate success.

Change does not sell itself. It makes stakeholders anxious, and has to be sold to them. They anticipate expense, disruption, uncertainty and mistakes that may make their organisation worse off. Change can go wrong, and most often goes wrong when people are not used to it, and do not possess the skillset it requires.

When an organisation needs to implement change, it must ensure that its people are prepared. Kotter *et al* itemise six key techniques for managing change: 1) Education and commitment 2) Participation and involvement 3) Facilitation and support 4) Negotiation and agreement 5) Manipulation and co-optation 6) Implicit and explicit coercion.

A given stakeholder might be:

- Change-loving – biased towards the potential benefits.
- Change-neutral – perfectly rational in their judgements.
- Change-averse – biased towards potential costs.

Egan suggests categorising stakeholders according to their relationship to you (as the change sponsor or leader) as much as the change itself. In this way, stakeholders might be:

- Partners – supporters of your change.
- Allies – supporters, if given encouragement.
- Fellow travellers – it suits their purposes to go along with you.
- Fence-sitters – who are not clear on what they want to do.
- Loose cannons – who may obstruct you at random, despite having no interest in the change.
- Opponents – who oppose the change, but not you.
- Adversaries – who oppose both you and your change.
- Bedfellows – who support the change, but do not trust you.
- Voiceless – who cannot influence anything however they feel.

Stakeholder communications

Each type of stakeholder should have their own communications plan. Simple, bite-sized statements may work well for those in more senior levels of the organisation, but greater detail may be needed for others, especially where they perceive they might have to change what they do. The overall plan should demonstrate that each stakeholder and all organisational levels have been considered appropriately. Circumstances will dictate the formality and methods to use with each individual stakeholder.

Stakeholder awareness of the issues is a prerequisite, but any programme also needs to address purpose, goals, benefits, and how stakeholders personally may be affected. There needs to be a facility for interaction at every point of communication to draw in feedback from the stakeholders.

There will be occasions when formal presentations and reports must be made to stakeholders. Some stakeholders will be influential enough to demand them and high-status enough to expect them. Presentations and reports are most useful when they are timely, accurate, and complete. It is important that reporting is inclusive and consistent.

Presenting strategic sourcing plans to stakeholders

A central part of stakeholder communication and involvement will be the formal presentation of the category strategic sourcing plan. It should contain the following sections.

- Current situation
- Business requirements
- Strategic analysis and insight
- Options for change
- Recommended sourcing option
- Risk and contingency plan
- High-level implementation plan
- Cost-benefit analysis
- Next steps
- Appendices (as needed)

The presentation of the sourcing plan at the implementation meeting will do the most to secure buy-in and allow for the process to be mapped for the implementation of the strategy.

O'Brien provides some interesting and pertinent pointers about the plan in the context of its implementation and its presentation to stakeholders.

- It must go only to internal stakeholders because of its content.
- It will vary in depth and complexity depending upon the nature of the improvement exercise and the category change programme. O'Brien visualises these factors as a matrix to help decide how the plan should be pitched. Getting the general approach and tone right greatly improves the chances of buy-in.

- Its purpose is to get organisational and stakeholder sign-off, and ultimate agreement to the recommended course of action.
- It also provides documentary evidence of the journey through the category that can serve as an audit, support future change in the management of the category (and others), and provide a baseline against which to track the programme and the benefits it has realised.
- It should include all of the information we have itemised in one document, although it will have begun as many documents with individual purposes right from the start of the process.
- It will provide an excellent communication vehicle to stakeholders and customers across the organisation.
- Making the sourcing plan available on the organisation's intranet is a good way to present it to stakeholders across the organisation.
- Sign-off of the category management sourcing plan is critical to the entire process.

The sourcing plan lies at the heart of the implementation, but there is no point in handing it to others and expecting them to work to understand its complexity and the intricacies of what is to be achieved. These should be made apparent by you. This is especially so if stakeholders are not familiar with the topic of category management or the background to buying products and services. It is then necessary to produce the best means of communication for the planned timetable and activity surrounding the implementation. This is likely to include:

- Microsoft Project for the programme planning tool for the detail of the events and activities.
- PowerPoint to capture the best and most relevant points of the bigger sourcing strategy.

A 'brown paper plan' may also be helpful in drawing together the data from stakeholders and to record the critical paths of activity for the project.

OWN NOTES

12

OWN NOTES

CHAPTER 13

Mobilisation, Start-Up and Transition

Performance improvement

Benefits of performance measurement:

* A longer-term, strategic view on the organisation's supply needs
* A hand in shaping those needs such that they can be fulfilled in a more value-adding way
* The organisation of supply needs into categories that can be managed with the same strategy
* Developing the most appropriate relationship with each of the organisation's suppliers
* Enabling the organisation's systems and processes to be more efficient, effective and economical – that is, delivering greater value for money.

The category manager needs to **monitor the performance** of the organisation's contracts.

* **Service delivery** – use the key performance indicators (KPIs) defined in the contract (typically in the form of a service level agreement, SLA) to monitor and remedy non-performance against the agreed outcomes.
* **Benefits tracking** – measure, monitor and achieve the benefits identified in the sourcing plan. These include price, improvements to processes and systems, and environmental and social aspects.

The category manager is responsible for taking corrective action when suppliers fail to comply with their contracts. This includes price monitoring, CSR and sustainability monitoring and making sure all internal personnel are using the installed contracts; identify and address off-contract spend. The category manager is responsible for establishing and maintaining the supplier relationship.

The category manager is the hub for continuous improvement activity in the organisation. He or she must ensure opportunities are identified and progressed throughout the life of every contract. This will involve specification improvement, process improvement and knowledge sharing

13

Planning for the effective start-up of category plans

The *Supply Management* Guide to Strategic Sourcing suggests that organisations can be somewhat backwards-facing in implementing and embedding strategic sourcing and category management. They take their lead from their key strategic supplier relationships, key stakeholders, existing strategic business requirements – all facets of previous experiences, whereas the point is to move away from tried, tested but not necessarily true methods.

The Guide describes how organisations idealise Deming's cycle of Plan-Do-Check-Act (PDCA), but that in reality they follow a 'pDF cycle', with pitifully little planning, which leads to misdirected Doing (because we need to be seen to be doing something as quickly as possible – which is a performance culture issue), that means we spend the rest of our time Firefighting instead of learning and improving.

Category management is a project that needs to be planned. To begin with, the organisation spends its time looking around, trying to establish where it is. It will analyse what it finds and decide where instead it wants to be. It will then need to connect these two states with a map or a plan.

O'Brien suggests using a **Gantt chart** format that makes it clear what is being done when and by whom, the steps that lead into and spring from each activity, and the key milestones and events.

O'Brien describes a brainstorming-style process called **brown paper planning**. The category team gets together with large quantities of paper and post-it notes and jointly brainstorms an end-to-end process that can then be operationalised as, for example, more sophisticated software-based representations.

The category project may be conceived on the assumption that certain other appropriate structures and resources are in place. O'Brien highlights: 1) Executive endorsement 2) Governance structure 3) Performance measurement and tracking mechanisms 4) Reporting structures 5) Communications structures 6)   Information technology infrastructure.

The category management project will be a collection of plans – each category will have its own plan and these category plans will need to be co-ordinated with a **programme project plan**. This outlines which categories are being worked on when and why. It directs resources as appropriate, so it may be politic to prioritise those categories where although the wins are not substantial, they will be quick, high-profile and garner or reinforce support for the process as a whole.

O'Brien says that it is typical for organisations to work on about five categories at any one time. Once a sourcing strategy is approved, its implementation must be planned. Here is a situation where detailed planning *is* needed, and the level of detail should be deep enough to enable all necessary management, monitoring and control processes.

Miles discusses six 'speed brakes' or reactive forces in organisations that hamper change. In ordinary circumstances these brakes have no significant effect on performance, but during the turbulent, transformative change that category management brings about, they resist the bold and rapid change required. They prevent the process performing well. If category management is to get off to a good start, then it must find ways to loosen these brakes. The brakes need to be released in a particular sequence for best effect.

- Cautious management culture
- Business-as-usual management processes
- Initiative gridlock
- Recalcitrant executives
- Disengaged employees
- Loss of focus during execution

Mobilising start-up and transition

Mobilisation means making ready to implement the category management approach. All mobilisation begins with a review of where the category management project is (in practical terms), and the stages of the process yet to be completed. There are elements of organisation, motivation and leadership to this, and procurement will be expected to provide all of these.

In order to ensure appropriate probity, contractual control, and specific delivery, it is important to finalise the actual contractual arrangements that have resulted from the tendering or approach to market and selection phase. The details concerned here will include not only the contractual terms and conditions upon which the business will be based, but also the agreed specification(s), timescale(s), installation or commencement of service arrangements, transition plans, pricing terms – ie all the operational aspects

Depending upon the prevailing constraints on contract extension there needs to be a suitable approach to **continuous improvement** in the contract. O'Brien suggests that continuous improvement should be targeted in value, quality, performance, price, process, efficiency, innovation – indeed any factor that we have already seen to flow from the business requirements and value levers.

Continuous improvement is embedded in the latter or last stages of all strategic sourcing and category management processes. Within category management, continuous improvement is based on continually evaluating and analysing market position, identifying opportunities for improvement, and designing and implementing appropriate changes in response. This implies that after the initial category management revolution, there is a default steady state of incremental improvements or protections from losses in performance.

Transition arrangements

Transition is the changeover from one supplier to another, from one contractual arrangement to another, or the continuation of an existing arrangement on a different basis. Transition will probably follow either a competition-based approach to market or a negotiation with an existing supplier that results in substantial operational differences.

The management of the transition should have been set out in the initial contract agreement in the form of **exit clauses** and arrangements that oblige the outgoing supplier to prepare a strategy for exiting.

The procurement function should make a **process map** of all organisational stakeholders who impact on or are impacted by the supply concerned so as to facilitate efforts to keep user and stakeholder experiences in line with their expectations. Once there is a map, the new contract introduction process can be designed.

If transition is not mapped appropriately, and communicated well in advance, there may be a tendency for users to procure off-contract, resulting in lower-quality procurement and diluting the intended benefits of the category process. There will also be confusion; stakeholders will not know what to expect or do, and this will result in poor performance.

The **handover** from the outgoing to the incoming supplier can be a high-risk period that, if mis-managed, can result in poorer service levels and worsened relationships with both suppliers. The suppliers may incur off-contract costs that are attributable to the organisation that they then seek to recoup.

Just as the outgoing supplier should have an exit strategy, so too the incoming supplier should have an entry strategy, and it is up to the organisation to agree these with the suppliers concerned and co-ordinate the two so that they interlock. Ideally, there should be an agreed period of overlap where the two suppliers work alongside each other

The exit strategy preparation and handover periods should be long enough for an orderly, well thought through, co-operative transition to take place. It is good practice for the exit strategy to be prepared early in the contract as an exit may be forced before the contract end date.

All conversations in the process should be three-way: the outgoing supplier can feel reassured they are not being misrepresented; the incoming supplier can feel reassured they are not walking into a mess; the organisation can feel reassured that all the elements of transition are happening to its satisfaction. Some exits are antagonistic and forced; acrimonious (litigious) transitions must be managed carefully.

OWN NOTES

13

OWN NOTES

CHAPTER 14

Managing Contracts and Suppliers

Responsibilities for contract management

Ultimate responsibility for contract management *should* lie with the procurement function. It is here that the signature for the contract responsibilities sits for the organisation, and it is here that changes to the contract are sanctioned, controlled and made.

However, depending on the nature of the organisation and the management and financial delegations for expenditure, there may be different attitudes and freedoms in existence within the organisation. Strategic contracts and those of high value are likely to be held in procurement's control in terms of the law, but in terms of everyday management there will be in practice processes aligned through the organisation that permit actions by operational resources and users to utilise services and goods from the contracts or frameworks deployed across the organisation. Such processes must be known and communicated to ensure financial probity, contract compliance, and benefits realisation across the organisation.

A contract manager's primary responsibilities are as follows.

- Participating, as necessary, in developing the specification and approach to the supply market. Contract administration must be considered during this process.
- Monitoring the supplier's progress and performance to ensure provision conforms to the contract requirements.
- Managing any organisational resources used in contract performance.
- Authorising payments consistent with the contract terms.
- Exercising remedies, as appropriate, where a supplier's performance is deficient.
- Resolving disputes in a timely manner.
- Documenting significant events.
- Maintaining appropriate records.

The number of people involved in managing a given contract will depend on its size, level of risk and complexity. Roles and responsibilities must be clear.

Plans, policies and procedures are an integral part of the specification. Contract administration likewise must be part of the specification. Planning for contract administration requires the contract manager to know, for example: expected outcome measures, costs, contract performance, acceptance and rejection terms and rights, contract dates and complete addresses.

The contract manager leads and arranges **post-award discussions** between the contract team at the organisation and the corresponding team at the supplier to fill out and finalise operational detail and ensure all parties are clear and aligned on how the contract will play out.

Once contract and sourcing arrangements are in place and operational, there must be an **examination of performance** to ensure that desired benefits are achieved and the performance envisaged from suppliers is met. There is a risk that once a contract is won, work on the sourcing project will be non-compliant or slow, or may even stop, so appropriate systems and governance must be in place to ensure the delivery of the contract.

Operational performance

Wheaton says that all organisations must quantify and **manage their risks** effectively in order to be successful over time. When dealing with suppliers, there are substantial risks. Most organisations recognise that these risks exist, but do not take sufficient steps to manage them effectively. By measuring and monitoring supplier performance on an ongoing basis, organisations can realise some significant benefits.

In setting out to **measure suppliers and manage relationships**, there must be a clear set of objectives and limits and boundaries around the process, involvement of stakeholders and time spent, and so on.

The **supplier relationship management programme** should designate the key stakeholders who will be involved in determining suppliers' performance levels and assessing improvements, and should specify the resources and processes required to do this. These things will be required to obtain buy-in and senior management support.

Wheaton suggests that the goals set for supplier relationship management and the measurement undertaken to support performance improvements must be aligned between a supplier and the goals and strategy of the organisation. Unless this is done, the supplier relationship programme will be at best less effective, and may result in wasted resources.

Relationships between organisations depend on the nature and extent of the business they conduct and attitudes they bring to it. Closer co-operation, once contracted, in some respects allows better understanding of the provision required, improved efficiencies and effectiveness, and also enhanced understanding of the parties' objectives. Caution must be adopted in this regard, however, as there are always contractual boundaries and conflicted interests between contractual parties, however collaborative their relationship.

Performance expectations and targets should be clearly defined, specific, and measurable, and should include a timeline. The choice of measures should directly relate to the organisation's corporate approach, its specific strategic goals and objectives, and the operational targets it is trying to meet. Everything should align.

Those metrics that are of critical importance to the organisation should be developed into **key performance indicators** (KPIs). It is important to work with the suppliers involved when developing these measures so as to determine whether they will be measurable and the most valid for the purpose sought.

There will be a number of tasks that the organisation and its suppliers can undertake, and tools that they can develop, to facilitate performance tracking, including information infrastructure, programme management, supplier lifecycle management and contract management.

Obtaining feedback from stakeholders

Stakeholder feedback must be captured and used as an evaluation mechanism to be fed into the supplier relationship management process and through the measurement indices. Circumstances will dictate the formality and methods you use with each individual stakeholder.

Stakeholder satisfaction must be fed back to the organisation continually so that it can understand how its actions are being received. There are three purposes in this: prediction and control, mutual understanding and critical reflection.

Without feedback mechanisms, stakeholders of any type, and indeed the organisation itself, will not be able to feed back any complaints, concerns or problems. The organisation will not be a *learning organisation.*

Category managers and sourcing specialists will gather information for the purpose of evaluating and measuring supplier performance through a variety of methods. There are costs involved in constant measurement and in obtaining feedback from stakeholders. Organisations must decide how and when it benefits them to use these methods.

Wheaton provides guidance for managing the supplier performance aspect of the supplier relationship and performance improvement programme, saying that the actual supplier evaluation must be structured in such a way that it produces information and data that can actually be used to make a decision.

Benchmarking performance

A **benchmark** is a standard against which something is compared. There are many definitions of **benchmarking** in business, but they all involve making comparisons with other organisations, then learning the lessons those comparisons provide. The purpose of benchmarking is to highlight differences in specific parameters examined between your organisation and others that you have chosen to aspire to or compete with in the market place to allow improvements in performance to be made for competitive advantage to be gained.

There must be a coherent methodology practised over time to ensure consistency of measurement. It can be difficult to establish the 'right measures' and the right approach to this to gain data to measure. Operational measures with input and output data or those pertaining to financial information will be easier to compile and assess, but will also reveal less interesting information about the overall direction and performance of the organisation. Less factual and more subjective data is useful, but less tangible and may relate to the impressions of customers, which is what brings and sustains business over time.

Creating performance improvements

Hammer and Champy relate a number of useful insights in relation to benchmarking.

'The first step is to map the process, because you can't improve anything if you can't define it.'

'You set objectives, establish milestones, then measure yourself against those milestones. It is no different from bringing a product to market, and it must be taken just as seriously.'

'Once you make the step forward, if you don't have earlier measurements, you can't do a comparison. Having some kind of scorecard as we went along might have accelerated succeeding projects.'

Commonly shared and consistent measurements can help organisations focus their resources, identify performance problems, develop strategies for supply chain improvements, and determine the total cost of ownership involved in given supply relationships, products, even entire supply chains.

Gordon suggests that four key strategies are common to the organisations achieving the greatest return from their supplier performance measurement initiatives.

- Tracking the performance of a broader portion of the supply base
- Standardising supplier performance measurement procedures across the organisation
- Collaborating with suppliers on performance metrics, reporting, and improvements
- Automating key supplier performance measurement activities

Gordon proposes a seven-step process for developing and deploying supplier assessment. Following the performance assessment it should be clear what actions are necessary to enhance or improve performance.

OWN NOTES

OWN NOTES

CHAPTER 15

Performance Measurement

Capturing data

Data gathering and analysis are key processes in effective strategic sourcing and category management. They must be continuous. An effective monitoring, research and analysis function will track category developments as well as individual contract performance to provide strategic insights and keep the organisation in touch with best practice.

All relevant data must be gathered. This will come from within the organisation and from the suppliers themselves. It is up to the category manager to specify what they need both during the sourcing phase with the supplier and when internal systems are being designed and installed, then later in encouraging colleagues to comply with them.

Data gathering is pointless without **analysis.** The organisation should aim to develop insights as to how category sourcing plans and contracts can be enhanced by identifying value for money and continuous improvement opportunities and identifying whether plans and contracts are delivering the required performance by reviewing organisational consumption behaviour, including off-plan and off-contract spend.

Category management entails step-changes. Gap analysis is vital. Keep contract renegotiation or cancellation as a live option during delivery if goals are not met or if substantially better ones could be achieved in other ways (even after allowing for compensation to the current supplier).

The category manager must continually undertake research that ensures the information for decisions is as complete and up-to-date as possible. This will include supply market price monitoring, benchmarking, industry best practice monitoring.

Effective, continuous, accrued and **milestone** benefits tracking ensures that intended outcomes are prioritised, and so have the best chance of being achieved. It helps mitigate the risk that value may be leaking away unnoticed, as may happen with traditional contract management.

All benefits should be tracked, quantitative and qualitative. As a category manager, you may apply the following example framework.

- **Specify the method** by which benefits tracking will take place.
- **Communicate the baseline** for price and non-price benefits and how incremental changes will be measured.

15

- **Communicate with suppliers** regarding the details of the benefits tracking process
- **Collect data** from supplier and departmental user-managers.
- **Verify data** and conduct an analysis.
- **Report** to stakeholders.

A vital part of data collection will be consistency. A key problem in data collection is the time that it takes for data to be created and submitted. Both these problems can be addressed through the use of **templates**.

Creating performance measures

O'Brien asserts that benefits measurement and tracking is critical so that benefits are reported. 'A benefit', he states, 'is only real when it has been realised and is clearly visible on the bottom line.'

- When a category management project is started, the benefits discussed are *projected* benefits
- As the sourcing strategy is generated, the benefits change status to become *anticipated* benefits.
- Then they become *actual* once negotiations have taken place, probably after appropriate market approaches have been made, competitive or otherwise.
- A benefit can only finally be said to be *real* when it is *complete*, ie the cash is in the bank.

Tracking benefits requires the recognition of these four stages of benefits development and realisation. Tracking benefits is a collaborative approach where the finance function supports the method of tracking and measuring the performance improvements attributed to suppliers and the implementation of category management.

Strategic sourcing and category management are *proactive* activities. The organisation takes control of its categories and engages proactively with stakeholders and supply markets. This is reflected in the strategic way in which they frame the benefits they track.

- Productivity
- Resiliency
- Precision
- Responsibility
- Revenue and performance

Dashboards

The *Supply Management* Guide suggests starting with a spend dashboard. It claims this gives instant visibility, assists with a variety of business decisions, and supports sourcing plan creation. It suggests the key areas are:

- Categorised spend
- Contract compliance
- Supplier concentration or supplier tail
- Levels of process improvement

- Interactive spend by business area.

A dashboard can be operationalised in a variety of ways, but must be optimised for usability. It should be dense, with a consistent design. Information should be presented so that it is easy to grasp and use. A dashboard should group like metrics together. The information will be 'live' – it changes in as close to real time as possible – so the dashboard should 'stamp' the information it provides with a time and date.

Reviewing improvements

Once there is a mechanism in place to periodically collect performance data from suppliers, the next step is to **review** the performance improvements. Ideally, the format that the data is in should lend itself to comparison and analysis. The data should also be in a format that can be quantified and scored. Many organisations use a supplier scorecard for this. Moreover, data from different types of assessments (eg internal surveys, external surveys, site visits) should be incorporated into the analysis.

Most large organisations have many strategic suppliers and lots of data, it is almost impossible to obtain, organise and review data and improvements systematically.

Supplier performance management is more than simply obtaining data on suppliers. It reflects the organisation's strategy and is a comprehensive approach to managing its supply base. It seeks to identify and mitigate risks in an attempt to boost overall profitability. It often involves performance assessments, supplier scorecards, periodic reviews of supplier data, and supplier development. It also includes a continuous improvement culture aimed at the performance of its supply base and at procurement outcomes.

Harris identifies a number of barriers and areas of organisational low performance that prevent organisations from fully realising the potential of their strategic sourcing and category management initiatives.

Training and development. Training and development is piecemeal, and focused on crossing hurdles and ticking boxes with lower-level staff. Senior staff are expected to arrive at organisations in an off-the-shelf manner, and require no development by the organisation. Consequently, senior decision making is a product of the disjointed talents, education and experience of these people.

Fully deployed category strategies. Categories often have many existing contracts in force within them when they are first designed and implemented. As a consequence, the organisation is never able to act cohesively, nor make the most of its aggregated spending power in its markets.

Fully developed and deployed e-procurement. Many organisations are behind the times in exploiting the potential of internet technologies and techniques. They have yet to build up institutionalised understanding and trust of even, in internet terms, established practices.

15

Management of indirect spend decision-making. Indirect spend, because it cuts across departmental and functional responsibilities, is handled by people with the status and hierarchical authority to act in that way, and not by procurement specialists who may lack the power to assert their expertise in these situations.

Contract compliance. Compliance is an issue of power, politics, trust, personal relationships and ego. Once the supply chain management function has contracts in place, agreed at the corporate centre and intended to be used by the entire organisation, some people will still make avoidable off-contract purchases.

Properly developed market analysis. Many organisations produce narrow, incomplete market analyses. They have the attitude that so long as some widely recognised tools have been applied, then everyone will agree the job has been done. It is a 'contractual obligation' approach. The organisation needs to be thorough and inquisitive

Fully integrated cross-functional involvement. While responsibility for sourcing may devolve to sourcing specialists, all parts and levels of the organisation are stakeholders in sourcing, and sourcing specialists should be active in all parts and levels of the organisation aligning their activities with everyone's goals and needs. The organisation needs to be fully joined up.

Total cost. Few organisations genuinely assess end-to-end total costs. Total costs begin when an input is first being considered – the cost of working with a market is a part of the cost of processing a given input – and spread out wide into forecast reliability, cross-border operations, performance management, reputational and repeat customer purchase implications, before finally narrowing down again into disposal. Benefits are not always properly assigned to costs,

Market-integrated pricing. Organisations do not necessarily use all of the leverage available to them in negotiating prices. 'Market' price reflects a wide variety of factors.

OWN NOTES

OWN NOTES

CHAPTER 16

Risk, Volatility and Exits

Dealing with supply chain risk

O'Brien recommends a structured approach to risk management that encompasses contingency planning, whether this means allowing for uncertainty or preparing for disaster. Risk management in the category management context is about highlighting, assessing and managing the likely risks and issues inherent in the disruptive process of adopting strategic sourcing and category management approaches.

Risk and vulnerability are connected ideas. **Vulnerability** is the susceptibility to adverse events and trends; **risk** is the characterisation of the likelihood and impact of those events and trends.

Resilience in supply chains describes the ability and time needed to recover the supply chain's original shape and level of performance (or perhaps even a better one) following a disruption. It implies a capacity to absorb and bend with impact, and to bounce back. There are connotations of flexibility and adaptability.

Robustness is often used interchangeably with resilience, which is not quite correct. Christopher and Peck note that this is more the opposite of vulnerability in that it is the resistance that the supply chain offers up in the face of risk so as to stay in its current shape. A robust supply chain might not be resilient (once broken it stays broken), and *vice versa*.

Organisations are always open to risk. Sound risk management procedures will identify the **inherent risks** in their activities. These are the exposures arising from specific risks before any actions have been taken to reduce them. **Residual risk** is the remaining exposure arising from a specific risk after all feasible action has been taken to manage it.

The organisation will make its decisions based on subjective **risk perception**, the personal view or opinion of the likelihood of a risk occurring and the impact it will have. You need to bring your supply chain risk perceptions as close as you can to reality.

Risk analysis should be as detailed as is worthwhile. Often organisations begin with a **coarse** or **preliminary risk analysis** to establish a crude risk picture for relatively modest effort. The purpose of this will be to filter risks into degrees of seriousness for further investigation. The risk analysis will deconstruct its subject into all reasonable sub-elements.

Sadgrove develops the **risk mapping approach**, using simple, qualitative categories for the severity of impact (Insignificant, Minor, Serious, Catastrophic) and the probability of

16

91

occurrence (Very unlikely, Improbable, Quite probable and Certain/Very probable). Risks can then be plotted on a simple grid.

Other risk matrix tools seek to quantify the risk. Karlof *et al* suggest a simple risk matrix based on the probability × consequence formula. Probability is expressed as a percentage and consequences are expressed as a number from 1 to 10 (1 being a negligible consequence and 10 being a catastrophic consequence). Another risk scoring approach would be simply to allocate numerical scores for likelihood, from very low (1) to very high (5), and impact from insignificant (1) to catastrophic (5), say.

Christopher and Peck describe five types of risk grouped into three categories – internal to the organisation, external but still in its supply or value chain, and environmental: process risks, control risks, supply risks, demand risks and environmental risks.

Risk management is designed to minimise losses and damage, both in the present and in the future, which in the case of the supply chain function may stem from supply failure or disruption, lack of resources, breakdowns in stakeholder relationships, or withdrawal of the organisation's licence to operate.

Risk management should not become **risk aversion.** The *systematic* management of risk, and the *confidence* it provides, are crucial in enabling innovation.

Risk identification is the process of asking 'what could go wrong?' It should be an ongoing process, as the organisation's **risk profile** may continually change, presenting new risks. A comprehensive list of identified risks should be compiled in a **risk register.**

Risk assessment or evaluation is the appraisal of the probability and significance of identified potential risk events: ie 'how likely is it and how bad could it be?'

Quantifying its risks allows an organisation to prioritise planning and resources to meet the most severe ones, and to set defined risk thresholds at which action on an issue will be triggered. Risk management strategies ('what can we do about it?') are often classified as the **Four Ts: Tolerate, Transfer or spread the risk, Treat or mitigate the risk, Terminate**

In any case, the organisation will need to make **contingency plans** to counter high-impact risks: eg alternative courses of action, alternative sources of supply, workarounds and fall-back positions ('what will we do if?').

Adjusting for volatility

Christopher *et al* suggest that most supply chain management models reflect the stable environments in which they were developed, and that those environments are increasingly unlikely to persist. **Volatility** is susceptibility to or predisposition for sudden, significant change. Organisations have typically addressed supply chain volatility with **dynamic flexibility**. Dynamic flexibility creates an efficient supply chain. It acts to return the supply chain quickly to its lowest cost state.

Structural flexibility anticipates rather than reacts to volatility. The inference is that managing for volatility is a truer supply chain perspective than managing for cost: the entire point of a supply chain is to supply; seeking efficiencies that erode the surety of supply is counter-productive.

A **disaster recovery plan** (DRP) is a documented process or set of procedures to recover and protect an organisation's operational infrastructure in the event of a disaster. Disasters can be the result of deliberate attacks (eg cyber crime) or freak natural occurrences (eg extreme weather), or any shade of targeting and premeditation in between.

The disaster recovery plan must be logical and well structured, and must include all of the organisation's operations that are likely to be impacted by disruptive events. It must be easily understood and must provide clear directions. It must be kept up to date. The plan's content tends to divide between background information and instructions.

The organisation's staffing, structure and hierarchy following any disaster and during any recovery will possibly be specific to those turbulent conditions and last only until normal operation is restored. The organisation may make extensive use of task teams, with precise and narrow responsibilities. Each team should have a designated leader and deputy. These people provide the necessary leadership and direction in developing their team's section of the plan and in carrying out their responsibilities during a disaster. Each team should be resourced according to the criticality of the asset they safeguard.

Creating exit arrangements

Contracts have pre-planned exits, or at least they should. Not all exits will be planned, however.

The first step in determining what needs to be done is to fully understand the existing arrangements with the provider with which we are closing our association. This may not be as straightforward as it sounds. Our original contract with them may have been in place for many years, and there may have been many subsequent modifications to it. Some, hopefully all, will have been recorded formally, in writing, but some may have been transacted through actions, norms or habits, or agreed verbally. There may be a lot of work that needs to be done to map the current arrangements.

We need to understand the impact, both operational and legal, of severing our relationship with the provider.

We need a clear understanding of exactly why we want to exit our arrangement with a provider as this will impact on the strategy and approach we take in managing the exit. For example, is it because of poor performance? Cost reduction? Insourcing? Or has the contract come to its natural end and a new provider won the business? Each scenario will have a different impact on the outgoing provider, the incoming provider, and our organisation.

These considerations all point to the need for a structured decision and planning process that will adapt the organisation's exit management procedures to each fresh situation so as to create the most effective and efficient result possible within the given timeframe and circumstances. An unplanned exit is not automatically a crisis, but it can be made into one if it is mishandled.

Organisations may be scared to contemplate an exit. They believe it to be so tricky that they avoid actively managing and monitoring suppliers because they know that if they discover something that they need to act upon, then they will be duty-bound to act. For them, it is better not to know.

The **termination notice** (the formal, contractual document that begins the process) should include the following elements.

- A description of the exact services included in the termination (including processes, sites and territories)
- A description of liabilities involved
- Details of transition arrangements
- A timetable with significant milestones
- Details of the manager in charge of the exit programme and any other necessary contacts
- Reporting requirements

OWN NOTES

OWN NOTES